silk flower
style

Sylvia Hague

A QUANTUM BOOK

Published in 2012 by Search Press Ltd.
Wellwood, North Farm Road,
Tunbridge Wells
Kent TN2 3DR

This book is produced by
Quantum Publishing
6 Blundell Street
London
N7 9BH

Care should be taken when using any of
the products recommended in this book,
or when following any of the technical
procedures. Follow manufacturer's
instructions and wear suitable protective
clothing and eyewear, where applicable.
Neither the author, copyright holders, nor
publishers of this book can accept legal
liability for any damage or injury sustained.

ISBN: 978-1-84448-829-2

QUMSSFF

Printed and bound in Singapore

Publisher: Sarah Bloxham
Managing Editor: Julie Brooke
Writer: Caroline Smith
Copy Editor: Judith Samuelson
Project Editor: Samantha Warrington
Assistant Editor: Jo Morley
Design: Dave Jones and Louise Turpin
Photographer: Simon Pask and
Elizabeth Zeschin

silk flower
style

Sylvia Hague

Search Press

CONTENTS

INTRODUCTION

I've loved working with silk flowers for many years, and during that time the quality of the blooms available has become so perfectly detailed and botanically correct that it is often hard to tell the difference between them and the real thing. The beauty of these lifelike silk flowers has inspired me to create some glorious arrangements for many different settings and many different occasions.

Silk flowers allow you to bring the beauty of nature in to your own home and to enjoy it all year round. And, as well as being beautiful, silk flowers give you the chance to create gorgeous floral arrangements that will last forever.

The range of silk flowers on offer today is amazing, as the varieties you can see at www.silkflowersbysylvia.com testify. In this book I've used those blooms that appeal most to me, and that work best in the types of displays that I like to create. However, we all have our own favourites – and our own sense of style – so whatever your taste, and whatever arrangement you wish to create, there is a wealth of silk flowers available from which to choose.

I hope this book inspires you to explore the beauty of silk flowers, and to bring their everlasting charm and colour in to your own home.

Sylvia Hague

GALLERY OF ARRANGEMENTS

In this book, you will find 22 stylish silk flower arrangements. Some chapters feature stunning displays to brighten up and enhance your home, while others contains arrangements designed with celebrations in mind. On these pages you will find snapshots of each gorgeous display.

The beautiful silk flower arrangements featured in this book offer something for everyone. They range in size from the small and simple Spring Collection on page 59, to the magnificent Wedding Top Table on page 104. You'll find an array of different styles – from the elegantly architectural Perfect Pompons on page 92, through to the wild and countrified Meadow Posy on page 78. There's a marvellous mix of colours from which to choose: you'll find bold and dramatic hues, such as the stunning red of Oriental Magic (see page 84); delicate colours, such as the calming Romantic Blues on page 81; and subtle shades and interesting combinations, as selected for the sumptuous Heart of the Home on page 56.

HEART OF THE HOME *pages 56–58*

POPPIES AND PINCUSHIONS *pages 59-61*

THE SPRING COLLECTION *pages 62-63*

LOVELY LAVENDER *pages 64–65*

FRESH GREENS *pages 66–67*

ELEGANT ORCHIDS *pages 68–70*

WILD AT HEART *pages 71–73*

WHITE DELIGHT *pages 74–77*

MEADOW POSY *pages 78–80*

ROMANTIC BLUES *pages 81–83*

ORIENTAL MAGIC *pages 84–86*

WINTER WARMTH *pages 87–89*

MY HEART'S EASE *pages 90–91*

PERFECT POMPOMS *pages 92–94*

CHRISTMAS WREATH *pages 95–97*

VALENTINE'S DAY BOUQUET *pages 100–101*

HEN PARTY BAGS *pages 102–103*

THE ANNIVERSARY DINNER *pages 104–105*

WEDDING TOP TABLE *pages 106-108*

INDIVIDUAL TABLE TOPPERS *pages 109-110*

BRIDAL BOUQUET *pages 110-111*

BABY SHOWER ROSES *pages 112–113*

MOTHER'S DAY TREAT *pages 114–115*

ANNIVERSARY AMARYLLIS *pages 116–117*

CHAPTER 1

Silk flower directory

In this directory of beautiful silk flowers and foliage, you will find essential information on the flower types available, as well as super tips on combining flowers to create stunning displays. As your knowledge and experience increases, you will be able to maximise the effect of each flower used.

SMALL SINGLE FLOWERS

Small flowers should not necessarily be reserved for smaller arrangements. Although individual blooms may be only small, many plants bear a mass of these flowers and can, therefore, make quite an impact. Small flowers can also add colour accents to a display, and introduce light and texture in the darker corners of an arrangement. And some smaller flowers are so beautiful that they themselves can be the focus of a display.

ANEMONE

FLOWERS Simple, open blooms, with soft, loose petals and dark, fluffy stamens. They come in shades of red, blue, purple, and also in white and pink.
LEAVES & STEMS Very thin, upright stems, with a few feathery leaves, clustered around the flower.
SIZE & IMPACT Medium-length stems with open flowers, about 5cm (2in) wide.
PERFECT FOR ... Simple, charming displays; used singly or with delicate foliage plants.

PINK RANUNCULUS

FLOWERS Tightly packed, rose-like flowerheads, composed of many delicate layers of pale pink and pale green petals. Often open flowers made with buds attached.
LEAVES & STEMS Thick, light green stems. Feathery leaves borne along the stems and near the flowers.
SIZE & IMPACT Flowers are 5–7.5cm (2–3in) across; the stems are short-to-medium in length.
PERFECT FOR ... Combining with wild flowers for a country style. Or with large blooms, such as roses and peonies.

SWEET PEA

FLOWERS Characteristic 'pea-flower' shape, with one upright petal and two lower petals. Flowers are white or in shades of pink, purple and blue.
LEAVES & STEMS Slender, upright stems bearing tendrils and just a few oval leaves.
SIZE & IMPACT Several flowers to a stem, each 2.5–3cm (1–1½in) across. Flowers are delicate but eye-catching.
PERFECT FOR ... Arrangements that mix traditional cottage-garden plants – such as roses and delphiniums – with plenty of foliage; or massed together in a glass vase.

PANSIES

FLOWERS Small, flat, five-petalled flowers, in white, purple shades, or wild-pansy colours – yellow and dark burgundy.

LEAVES & STEMS Short, fine stems; masses of relatively large, oval- or heart-shaped leaves with indented edges.

SIZE & IMPACT Each bunch bears many small flowers and leaves; one bunch provides plenty of flowers.

PERFECT FOR … Low arrangements, combined with larger flowers; use at the front of displays, angled outwards. Or, use alone planted in massed bunches in a single container.

PINCUSHION

FLOWERS Also known as scabious, these flowers are small but showy, with fluffy centres that are said to resemble pincushions. In white and shades of red, pink and blue.

LEAVES & STEMS Narrow, pointed leaves, borne low down on the smooth, slender stems.

SIZE & IMPACT Each stem bears two–to–three branching stems, with flowers presented in various stages of opening – from closed bud to fully open.

PERFECT FOR … Bringing light and texture to displays with strongly shaped flowers and foliage.

WAXFLOWER

FLOWERS Masses of tiny, cup-shaped flowers, in cream or greeny yellow, edged with red.

LEAVES & STEMS Wiry, thin, branching stems with lots of small, needle-like leaves.

SIZE & IMPACT Long stems with plenty of small flowers and leaves.

PERFECT FOR … Filling out displays with delicate notes of brighter colour and adding a feathery texture with the use of distinctive foliage.

CREAM RANUNCULUS

FLOWERS Many wide, thin petals, so tightly packed that the blooms resemble rose buds.

LEAVES & STEMS Thick, erect stems with slightly feathery, pale green leaves held near the flowers.

SIZE & IMPACT Distinctive flowers that work well when combined with lighter, frothier flowers.

PERFECT FOR ... Arrangements with a country-garden look; open, loose displays with a variety of other contrasting flowers and greenery.

LOVE-IN-A-MIST

FLOWERS Delicate blooms in shades of blue, pink, or in pure white. Each individual flower has a cluster of green, feathery stamens at the centre.

LEAVES & STEMS Thin, branching stems with pale green, feathery leaves.

SIZE & IMPACT Each stem bears several flowers; use to add height and interest at the back of displays.

PERFECT FOR ... Breaking up an arrangement that features large, strongly shaped flowers.

WILD CLEMATIS

FLOWERS Masses of tiny blue or white flowers with delicate, yellow-tipped stamens.

LEAVES & STEMS Long, slender, branching stems with an abundance of glossy, green, oval leaves.

SIZE & IMPACT Tall stems topped with multiple small flowers and contrasting leaves.

PERFECT FOR ... Combining together with larger single blooms that have strong, well-defined shapes; to soften an arrangement or to fill in a background.

BUTTERCUPS

FLOWERS Dainty, brilliant yellow flowers, each one made up of five, loosely open petals.

LEAVES & STEMS Delicate, many-branching stems that bear a few leaves towards the base.

SIZE & IMPACT Long stems that bear many small flowers, buds and also seedheads.

PERFECT FOR ... Wild-flower arrangements, combined with grasses and other country-style flowers. Ideal for introducing a light, but bright, dash of colour.

LARGE SINGLE FLOWERS

If you are putting together a grand, impressive display – for a table centrepiece, or a wedding decoration – then you may want to include some large single flowerheads among your selection. Strategically placed, larger flowers can act as focal points in your arrangement, and can create a dramatic impact when combined with a mass of greenery and sprays of smaller-sized flowers.

AMARYLLIS

FLOWERS Exotic-looking blooms, made up of large, soft petals. They are available in shades of red, orange, and magenta, and also in white.

LEAVES & STEMS Very thick, upright stems, without leaves attached.

SIZE & IMPACT Long stems and wide, open flowers make a genuine impact; ideal focal points.

PERFECT FOR … Elegant, eye-catching displays. Combine with foliage or use alone, en masse.

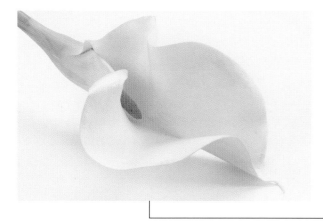

CALLA LILY

FLOWERS These distinctive flowers comprise a single 'petal' (a spathe) which encloses the protruding spadix. Available in white, cream and pinky maroon shades.

LEAVES & STEMS Long, slender, leafless stems.

SIZE & IMPACT Large flowers on tall stems. Ideal specimen blooms or as key plants in mixed displays.

PERFECT FOR … Combining with other exotics or with dark green foliage. Three to five lilies look stunning arranged in a glass vase with curly willow stems.

DAHLIA

FLOWERS Made up of many, tightly packed petals; available in both bright and subtle colours.

LEAVES & STEMS Strong, upright stems with dark green, serrated leaves.

SIZE & IMPACT Large and wide blooms but with a delicate look due to the multiple petals.

PERFECT FOR … Mixed arrangements, combined with other brightly coloured blooms and darker foliage. Use sparingly since they can dominate a display.

MAGENTA PEONY

FLOWERS Large, cup-shaped, double flowers available in a shade of shocking pink.

LEAVES & STEMS Slim, upright, branching stems that each bear several flowers; numerous spear-like, lobed leaves.

SIZE & IMPACT Tall stems with large, round flowers, 10–12.5cm (4–5in) wide.

PERFECT FOR ... Grand, imposing displays; use to establish the key colour in an arrangement.

PEONY BUD

FLOWERS Tightly packed, spherical flower buds, made up of overlapping circular petals; in graduated shades of pink, pure white and cream.

LEAVES & STEMS Slim branching stems that bear several buds and typical peony foliage. Flowering stems may also be combined with closed buds.

SIZE & IMPACT The buds are about 2.5cm (1in) across, borne on thin upright stems.

PERFECT FOR ... Combining with peony flowers or other large, open blooms – such as roses – for a natural look.

CREAM PEONY

FLOWERS Large flowers made up of many soft petals in a rich, deep shade of cream.

LEAVES & STEMS Slender, upright stems with dark green, many-lobed leaves.

SIZE & IMPACT Large and wide blooms 10–12.5cm (4–5in) across, borne on tall stems.

PERFECT FOR ... Mixed arrangements, combined with other cream-coloured flowers; they also work well as the single flower in a display when accompanied by foliage plants.

STRIPED PEONY

FLOWERS Many-petalled, cup-shaped flowers, with petals of blush pink streaked with a darker shade.

LEAVES & STEMS Slim, upright stems, with several dark green, lobed leaves.

SIZE & IMPACT Tall stems with two or three branches, each bearing a large flower about 7.5cm (3in) wide.

PERFECT FOR ... Displays that combine pink and white flowers, acting as an essential link between solid pink flowers and pure white blooms.

WHITE PEONY

FLOWERS Large cup-shaped, white flowers, with wide outer petals, and narrower, feathery inner petals. The red-tipped sepals underneath each flower add a note of colour.

LEAVES & STEMS Strong, upright stems. Dark green spear-like, lobed leaves.

SIZE & IMPACT Flowers measure 10–12.5cm (4–5in) across; the long stems can provide height at the back of a display.

PERFECT FOR ... White-only arrangements, especially mixed displays that feature large, dramatic blooms.

LILY

FLOWERS Exotic, luscious flowers, with long, protruding stamens. Often with flower buds attached for a slender contrast.

LEAVES & STEMS Strong, upright stems with long, dark green, spear-like leaves.

SIZE & IMPACT Notable, large blooms, about 10cm (4in) long, several to each tall stem.

PERFECT FOR ... Using alone or within special bouquets; use with care in mixed arrangements since they can dominate other flowers.

BURGUNDY HELLEBORE

FLOWERS Open flowers with five main outer petals and a cluster of small feathery petals and stamens at the centre. Also known as the Lenten rose.

LEAVES & STEMS Sturdy, upright stems, with a few narrow, serrated leaves.

SIZE & IMPACT Medium-length branching stems with several flowers, about 5cm (2in) wide, and small buds.

PERFECT FOR ... Combining with light green foliage or pale-coloured, frothy flowers.

WHITE HELLEBORE

FLOWERS Five-petalled, open flowers with yellow-tipped green stamens at the centre. The white petals are delicately speckled with green.

LEAVES & STEMS Thin, light green stems with a few narrow leaves directly below the flowers.

SIZE & IMPACT Short-to-medium-length stems with two-to-three flowers, about 5cm (2in) wide.

PERFECT FOR ... Combining with white and pale green flowers, such as viburnum, or as a foil to focal points.

POPPY

FLOWERS Large, soft, papery petals in white, red or shades of pink and mauve. With prominent stamens and ovary at the centre.

LEAVES & STEMS Thin, soft stems with one or two slightly ruffled leaves.

SIZE & IMPACT Large and wide blooms, about 10cm (4in) across, with a delicate appearance.

PERFECT FOR ... Mixed arrangements, combined with more strongly shaped flowers and the spiky foliage of grasses.

PURPLE TULIP

FLOWERS Oval, almost goblet-shaped flowers, made up of six wide petals.

LEAVES & STEMS Thick, slightly bending stems with long leaves borne at the very base of the stem.

SIZE & IMPACT Distinctive flowers, about 5cm (2in) long, borne singly on each stem.

PERFECT FOR ... Single flower arrangements, using one colour of tulip or combining tulips of several different colours. Also works well with other spring-flowering plants.

PARROT TULIP

FLOWERS Parrot tulips have slightly ruffled petals with fringed edges. The flowers are more open than standard tulips. Available in many shades.

LEAVES & STEMS Thick, glossy stems, bearing two long leaves at the base.

SIZE & IMPACT Each stem bears one large, open flower, about 15cm (6in) wide and 10cm (4in) long.

PERFECT FOR ... Arrangements that require a strong focal point; combine with smaller, more delicate blooms.

DOUBLE TULIP

FLOWERS Cup-like, slightly open flowers with several large petals. Available in several colours and with striped petals.

LEAVES & STEMS Long, slender stems, sometimes with sword-like leaves at the base.

SIZE & IMPACT Flowers are borne singly, measuring 5–7.5cm (2–3in) across and 5cm (2in) long. The striped flowers have maximum impact.

PERFECT FOR ... Mixing with other tulips or spring flowers. Combine the striped flowers with blooms of either colour.

WHITE TULIP

FLOWERS White, goblet-shaped flowers, made up of large inward curving petals.

LEAVES & STEMS Strong stems that curve at the flowerhead; long leaves are borne at the base of the stem.

SIZE & IMPACT Single flowers, about 5cm (2in) long, with a strong, well-defined shape.

PERFECT FOR ... Displays made up of different types of white flower and mixed foliage – such as cow parsley, white roses, narcissi and alliums.

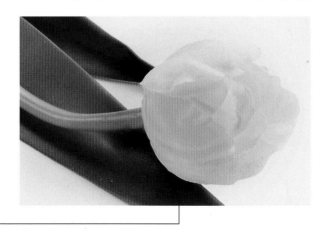

LARGE MULTIPLE FLOWERHEADS

Some blooms are made up of many small flowers that combine to appear as one flowerhead. The effect of such flowerheads varies: in some instances, the individual flowers are held in loose, open groups to provide an open, lacy look; in other situations, the small flowers cluster in to dense, compact flowerheads; while others feature larger individual flowers grouped together in long, tall flowerheads.

ANGELICA

FLOWERS Large, dome-shaped flowerheads, made up of clusters of extremely tiny individual flowers. These flowers are burgundy, tinged with purple or green.

LEAVES & STEMS Thick, upright stems, with several branches, and a few lobed leaves.

SIZE & IMPACT Very tall stems, with several flowerheads, 12.5–15cm (5–6in) across.

PERFECT FOR ... Adding height to the back or side of an arrangement without overpowering the other flowers.

CLEOME

FLOWERS Also known as the spider flower. Individual flowers have long, narrow petals and protruding stamens that give the blooms a spidery appearance.

LEAVES & STEMS Thick stems, with a few leaves below the flowerhead and a larger cluster further down.

SIZE & IMPACT Unusual flowers on tall stems. Flowerheads are about 15cm (6in) tall.

PERFECT FOR ... Combining with more exotic flowers, such as lilies and amaryllis.

COW PARSLEY

FLOWERS Flowerheads are shaped like upside-down umbrellas, and made up of clusters of very tiny white flowers.

LEAVES & STEMS Tall, upright, slightly ribbed stems with several small, green, serrated leaves.

SIZE & IMPACT Large flowerheads, about 10cm (4in) across, with a distinctive, frothy appearance.

PERFECT FOR ... Mixed arrangements, combined with strongly shaped flowers. They are deal for adding height and texture.

BURGUNDY HYDRANGEA

FLOWERS Flowerheads made up of small, but distinct, individual flowers in a deep, dusky burgundy colour, slightly tinged with green.

LEAVES & STEMS Short, thick stems; large, heart-shaped leaves with serrated edges.

SIZE & IMPACT Wide, slightly domed flowerheads, about 20cm (8in) across.

PERFECT FOR … Arrangements that combine a variety of different types of foliage with strong, architectural plants.

PINK HYDRANGEA

FLOWERS Small flowers in shades of pale pink, tinged with lime green at the centre.

LEAVES & STEMS Strong, upright stems, bearing one flowerhead. Several serrated, heart-shaped leaves.

SIZE & IMPACT Wide, rounded flowerheads of a distinctive shape and strongly shaped foliage.

PERFECT FOR … Mixing with country-garden flowers, such as ranunculi, anemones and pincushions.

WHITE HYDRANGEA

FLOWERS Flowerheads are made up of many small, white flowers with inward curving petals, borne on slender, red-tinged stems.

LEAVES & STEMS Short, strong stems, with dark green, heart-shaped leaves.

SIZE & IMPACT Single flowerheads on each stem, measuring 10–15cm (4–6in) tall.

PERFECT FOR … Arrangements that mix other large, multiple flowerheads, such as viburnums and lady's mantle.

AGAPANTHUS

FLOWERS Large flowerheads made up of many small, trumpet-shaped flowers, in shades of blue carried on straight delicate stems.

LEAVES & STEMS Slender, upright, leafless stems; the strap-like leaves are available separately.

SIZE & IMPACT Tall stems with single flowerheads, about 15cm (6in) wide.

PERFECT FOR … Striking, architectural displays, combined with other large flowers.

LADY'S MANTLE

FLOWERS Clusters of tiny, star-like flowers in lime green.

LEAVES & STEMS Thin upright stems. Fan-shaped leaves: the smaller leaves are borne near the flowers, the larger ones are lower down the stem.

SIZE & IMPACT Stems bear several branches, with several flowerheads, each about 5cm (2in) wide.

PERFECT FOR … Mixing with large, single flowers, such as peonies or roses. Or, place singly in a tall glass vase with strappy greenery or pussy willow stems.

ALLIUM

FLOWERS Large, spherical flowerheads made up of many, tiny, star-like flowers, in white or shades of purple and with pale green stamens.

LEAVES & STEMS Thick, erect, leafless stems; the leaves are available separately.

SIZE & IMPACT Distinctive flowerheads, about 15cm (6in) wide, borne singly on each stem.

PERFECT FOR … Large architectural displays, carefully combined with other alliums. Or, just place loose in a vase for a contemporary look.

PINK CYMBIDIUM ORCHID

FLOWERS Dramatic flowers, with pale pink outer petals and a deeper, richer pink tubular petal positioned in the centre.

LEAVES & STEMS Thick, upright stems with several small branches at the top that bear the flowers.

SIZE & IMPACT Showy blooms on flowerheads, measuring about 20cm (8in) long.

PERFECT FOR ... Mixing with other exotics or arranged in groups of several single orchids.

WHITE CYMBIDIUM ORCHID

FLOWERS Slender white outer petals, with a pink-speckled inner petal, and a browny yellow centre.

LEAVES & STEMS Thin, long stems with upper branches bearing flowers. Slim leaves at the base.

SIZE & IMPACT Exotic flowerheads, reaching up to 20cm (8in) long.

PERFECT FOR ... Elegant arrangements that use a few, carefully positioned stems to create an architectural display.

MULTICOLOURED MOTH ORCHID

FLOWERS Yellow outer petals, veined with magenta; shocking-pink and unusually shaped centre petals; yellow at the centre.

LEAVES & STEMS Slender, erect, branching stems; leaves available separately.

SIZE & IMPACT Tall stems with impressive flowerheads 15–20cm (6–8in) long.

PERFECT FOR ... Combining with simple foliage and other dramatically shaped blooms.

WHITE MOTH ORCHID

FLOWERS White outer petals; yellow-tinged inner petal, faintly flecked with magenta; yellow centres.

LEAVES & STEMS Slender, jointed stems bear flowerheads about 20cm (8in) long, interspersed with buds up to the tip.

SIZE & IMPACT Long stems that bear many small flowers, buds and seedheads.

PERFECT FOR ... Large, complex displays; used singly or in groups of several moth orchids.

DILL

FLOWERS Flat, yellow flowerheads, shaped like an inverted umbrella. Clusters of tiny, starry flowers are held up on slender branchlets.

LEAVES & STEMS Slim, slightly bending stems, with very fine, feathery leaves.

SIZE & IMPACT Delicate frothy flowers; their size – about 15cm (6in) wide – makes an impact.

PERFECT FOR … Adding height to large arrangements that use showy, but short, blooms.

QUEEN ANNE'S LACE

FLOWERS Delicate flowerheads, made up of tiny, frothy white flowers, clustered together in an umbrella shape.

LEAVES & STEMS Upright stems accompanied by a few serrated leaves.

SIZE & IMPACT Tall stems bear one multiple flowerhead, up to 15cm (6in) across.

PERFECT FOR … Creating texture and breaking up the outline of an arrangement comprised of large, strongly shaped flowers.

PALE GREEN VIBURNUM

FLOWERS Densely clustered, small green flowers make up the almost globular flowerheads.

LEAVES & STEMS Thin brown stems leading to pale green stems that bear the flowerheads; large, three-lobed leaves near the flowerheads.

SIZE & IMPACT Tall stems with abundant flowerheads and strongly shaped leaves.

PERFECT FOR … Combining with other multiple flowerheads or large, distinctive blooms.

WHITE VIBURNUM

FLOWERS Dainty, small white flowers are clustered together in to round flowerheads.

LEAVES & STEMS Long, thin stems with flower-bearing branches; plenty of lobed leaves.

SIZE & IMPACT Plenty of moderately sized flowerheads, each 7.5–10cm (3–4in) across.

PERFECT FOR … Mixed arrangements, combined with large, single flowers, such as roses and peonies for contrast.

SMALL MULTIPLE FLOWERHEADS

Blooms with multiple flowerheads are not always large; the smaller individual flowers can be grouped together to form relatively small flowerheads. But they are no less lovely for their lack of size. Some have a dainty, lacy appearance that can add a delicate touch to any display. Others have striking and boldly shaped flowerheads, that help give structure and form to an arrangement.

NARCISSUS

FLOWERS Clusters of small daffodil-like flowers – with trumpet-shaped centres and six outer petals – in white, cream or yellow.

LEAVES & STEMS Thick, upright stems, with three or four narrow, strap-like leaves attached at the base.

SIZE & IMPACT Flowerheads measure about 7.5cm (3in) across, borne at the top of the short stems.

PERFECT FOR … Using singly or combining with other spring-themed flowers.

SMALL ALLIUM

FLOWERS As with larger, pompon-like alliums, these miniature versions are globular clusters of small, dainty flowers. Available in white and shades of purple.

LEAVES & STEMS Slender, leafless stems.

SIZE & IMPACT Small flowers, about 2.5cm (1in) in diameter, borne singly on the thin stems.

PERFECT FOR … Mixing with flowers that have a delicate shape – such as Love-in-a-Mist or Verbena – to add some structure to a display.

COW PARSLEY BUDS

FLOWERS The budding flowers of cow parsley; the tightly packed buds form slightly fluffy pompons in white and pale purple.

LEAVES & STEMS Very fine, upright stems with many multiple-lobed leaves, in various green shades.

SIZE & IMPACT Plenty of very small flowerheads, less than 2.5cm (1in) across, borne on branching stems.

PERFECT FOR … Combining with cow parsley flowers, to add a new texture, or with larger single flowers, such as peonies or hellebores.

VERBENA

FLOWERS Clusters of small, five-petalled, purple flowers; at the centre of each cluster are a few developing seedheads.
LEAVES & STEMS Thin, branching stems with an abundance of very feathery leaves.
SIZE & IMPACT Flowers are 2.5–5cm (1–2in) wide and carried on several branching stems.
PERFECT FOR … Arrangements with a country-garden look; in combination with other delicate flowers, such as anemones or pincushions.

SMALL WHITE HYDRANGEA

FLOWERS A mass of tiny, white flowers, borne on delicate, pale green, individual stems.
LEAVES & STEMS Slender, upright stems adorned with a few, heart-shaped leaves with serrated edges.
SIZE & IMPACT Each stem bears one globe-like cluster, measuring 5–7.5cm (2–3in) across.
PERFECT FOR … Combining with multiple flowerheads, such as other hydrangeas or viburnums; or mixing with statement blooms, such as agapanthus and alliums.

SMALL PURPLE HYDRANGEA

FLOWERS A cluster of small flowers, mostly purple but some in pale green, tinged with red at the petal edge.
LEAVES & STEMS Short thick stems with four heart-shaped, serrated leaves placed directly below the flowerhead, creating a collar around the petals.
SIZE & IMPACT Flowerheads are about 10cm (4in) wide, but the leaves combine to make a greater impact.
PERFECT FOR … Creating small but distinct focal points in mixed displays, especially in shorter arrangements.

STAR OF BETHLEHEM

FLOWERS A cluster of small, but distinct, white flowers; each one displaying dark, yellowy-green stamens at the centre.
LEAVES & STEMS Short, flexible stems with a few strap-like leaves at the base.
SIZE & IMPACT Stems bear a single flowerhead, about 7.5cm (3in) across.
PERFECT FOR … Displays that mix several kinds of white flowers, with various different textures.

FLOWER SPIKES

Some silk flowers bear many distinct flowers on a single stem, arranged along the
length of the stem so that a long flower spike is formed. Such flowers carry blooms over a
considerable proportion of the stem, and are ideal when you want to include a line or strip
of colour in your arrangement. Flower spikes also allow you to add both height
and colour to larger displays.

FREESIA

FLOWERS Funnel-shaped flowers in various stages of
opening – buds, part-opened and fully open. Available in
bold and subtle shades, and also in white.

LEAVES & STEMS Short, slim, flexible stems with many
branches at the top that bear the flowers.

SIZE & IMPACT Flowers cover 10–12.5cm (4–5in) of each
individual stem for a dense block of colour.

PERFECT FOR … Displays with roses, narcissi, hyacinths or
peonies. Or use alone massed together in a tall vase.

PINK DELPHINIUM

FLOWERS Double flowers, with the outer petals in shades of
pink, and finished with tiny white petals in the centre.

LEAVES & STEMS Tall stems with flowers and closed buds
covering the top part; light green leaves below the flowers.

SIZE & IMPACT Tall stems with masses of flowers, each
2.5–5cm (1–2in) wide, covering 30cm (12in) of the stem.

PERFECT FOR … Combining with old-fashioned favourites,
such as honeysuckle and poppies, for a quintessential
cottage-garden look.

BLUE DELPHINIUM

FLOWERS Blue flowers with slightly curling, almost
translucent petals; in various stages of opening, including
closed buds.

LEAVES & STEMS Tall, upright stems with the greater part
bearing a mass of individual flowers. Leaves are divided
and finished with serrated edges.

SIZE & IMPACT Imposing flower spikes with an intense,
bright colour.

PERFECT FOR … Displays that feature other blue flowers,
such as agapanthus; ideal for adding height and colour.

HYACINTH

FLOWERS Individual flowers are trumpet-shaped, opening out at the mouth. Available in white and in shades of pink and blue.

LEAVES & STEMS Very thick, fleshy stems. Leaves are available separately.

SIZE & IMPACT Small individual flowers borne on conical spikes about 15cm (6in) long.

PERFECT FOR … Ideal on their own, as if planted in soil. Or grouped with other spring blooms.

GRAPE HYACINTH

FLOWERS Tiny, blue, droplet-like flowers borne in conical spikes. Also known as Muscari.

LEAVES & STEMS Thin stems, bearing single spikes; available attached to bulbs and with several narrow, strap-like leaves.

SIZE & IMPACT Short, thin stems and small flower spikes, 2.5–5cm (1–2in) long, of an intense blue colour.

PERFECT FOR … Using singly, or grouped together en masse for a dramatic display.

IRISH BELLS

FLOWERS The blooms consist of green calyxes with small, white flowers at the centre. Also known as Moluccella.

LEAVES & STEMS Long stems with the flower spike taking up most of the stem; no leaves.

SIZE & IMPACT Tall, but slightly drooping stems, with flower spikes 30–35cm (12–14in) long.

PERFECT FOR … Using as an alternative to foliage when you need to add more greenery, or to add height and an unusual texture to a display.

LAVENDER

FLOWERS Flower spikes formed by tiny, upward-pointing, purple petals that cluster around the stem.

LEAVES & STEMS Thin, slightly downy, silver-green stems. Clusters of silver-green, needle-like leaves towards the base.

SIZE & IMPACT Slender stems bear small, fine flower spikes that are a strong purple colour.

PERFECT FOR … Wild-flower arrangements, combined with cottage-garden-style plants and grasses. Or tie together in informal bunches for maximum impact.

ROSES

The variety of silk roses available is remarkable; so much so that they are worthy of their own grouping. Cottage-garden favourites, such as Old roses and Floribunda roses are widely available in natural shades. More modern varieties, including English roses and Tea roses, are offered in bold, striking colours, as are delicate miniature variations. All can be used to great effect in a number of different ways.

DARK RED TEA ROSE

FLOWERS Intense, dark-red roses, made up of many whorled petals – the classic rose to give as a love token.

LEAVES & STEMS Branching stems, complete with artificial thorns, buds and dark green, oval leaves.

SIZE & IMPACT Thick, slightly bending stems that bear one or two open flowers, up to 7.5cm (3in) across, and small buds.

PERFECT FOR ... Elegant, formal displays. Combine with dark-green foliage plants or light-green flowers for an interesting colour contrast.

BLUSH PINK ENGLISH ROSE

FLOWERS Flowers are made up of many, outward-curving petals in a very pale, blush pink. The petals fall open to reveal a cluster of yellow stamens.

LEAVES & STEMS Long, sturdy stems with thorns, bearing a few branches of oval leaves just below the flowers.

SIZE & IMPACT Large open flowers, 7.5–10cm (3–4in) wide on tall stems.

PERFECT FOR ... Combining with different rose types or other flowers in shades of pink.

WHITE FLORIBUNDA ROSE

FLOWERS Small, cup-shaped white roses, with many petals that open to reveal delicate yellow stamens.

LEAVES & STEMS Thick, thorned stems with multiple branches and plenty of dark green, serrated leaves.

SIZE & IMPACT A profusion of smaller roses, up to 5cm (2in) across, and rose buds. The abundance of foliage provides a contrasting backdrop to the white petals.

PERFECT FOR ... Displays that feature other types of white rose, or in mixed arrangements with other popular garden flowers.

APRICOT TEA ROSE

FLOWERS Large, pale apricot petals are whorled tightly together to form the flowers.

LEAVES & STEMS Thick, upright stems with thorns; serrated leaves are dark green and occasionally tinged with other autumnal colours.

SIZE & IMPACT Tall stems with single flowers, up to 5cm (2in) wide, sometimes with buds attached.

PERFECT FOR … Sophisticated displays; used singly or combined with other Tea roses in subtle shades.

WHITE MINIATURE ROSE

FLOWERS Cup-shaped, open flowers made up of many white, circular petals.

LEAVES & STEMS Short, thorned stems and small oval leaves. Each stem bears several branches and many flowers in various stages of opening.

SIZE & IMPACT Open flowers are small, up to 2.5cm (1in) across, but flowers and buds are borne in profusion.

PERFECT FOR … Displays made up of several miniature rose stems or mixed with love-in-a-mist or verbena.

PINK ENGLISH ROSE

FLOWERS A blousy-looking flower, with plenty of loosely arranged petals in subtle shades of a sugary pink.

LEAVES & STEMS Strong, upright thorned stems with glossy green, serrated, oval leaves.

SIZE & IMPACT Large blooms, up to 10cm (4in) wide, but with a delicate look due to the abundance of individual petals.

PERFECT FOR … Mixed arrangements, combined with other roses or pink flowers such as poppies and pincushions.

WHITE TEA ROSE

FLOWERS Tightly overlapping, white petals with a rich, creamy tinge; a few golden stamens visible at the centre.

LEAVES & STEMS Slender stems, with a few thorns and oval leaves held near the flower.

SIZE & IMPACT Medium-sized roses, about 5cm (2in) wide, borne singly or with a few buds.

PERFECT FOR ... Mixed displays of white flowers; combine with blooms of different shape and texture, such as cow parsley, Star of Bethlehem or viburnum.

PINK FLORIBUNDA ROSE

FLOWERS Flowers made up of many large, tightly whorled petals, in a charming and old-fashioned shade of pink.

LEAVES & STEMS Slim stems with many branches bearing many flowers in different stages of opening. Plentiful, serrated oval leaves.

SIZE & IMPACT Flowers are 5–7.5cm (2–3in) across, the stems are of short-to-medium length.

PERFECT FOR ... Using with other pink roses or mixing with frothy flowers, such as Queen Anne's lace, for a rural look.

MAGENTA TEA ROSE

FLOWERS Tightly packed, large petals that are mainly magenta but tinged with a pale orange for a distinctive colour contrast.

LEAVES & STEMS Slim, upright stems with few thorns and dark green, serrated leaves.

SIZE & IMPACT Medium-sized roses – up to 5cm (2in) wide – in a striking colour.

PERFECT FOR ... A focal point in mixed displays to make the most of the colour; combining with blooms in paler shades.

WHITE OLD ROSE

FLOWERS An old-fashioned garden rose with many loose and soft white petals; a delicate cluster of golden stamens at the centre.

LEAVES & STEMS Thick, erect stems with many serrated oval leaves, some tinged red.

SIZE & IMPACT Stems bear several flowers in various stages of opening. Fully open flowers are about 12.5cm (5in) across.

PERFECT FOR … Grand displays, combined with other showy flowers, such as hydrangeas, alliums or agapanthus.

PALE PINK TEA ROSE

FLOWERS Pale pink, almost mauve, petals with a faint yellow tinge at the base, all tightly packed together.

LEAVES & STEMS Strong, thorned upright stems with dark green, serrated oval leaves.

SIZE & IMPACT Medium-sized flowers – up to 5cm (2in) wide – borne singly, sometimes with buds.

PERFECT FOR … Any arrangement that combines blooms in subtle shades – cream, pale purple and apricot – for an understated but sophisticated look.

ROSE BUDS

FLOWERS Buds in various stages of opening, from fully closed, to just emerging and partly open. With obvious green sepals placed below the blooms.

LEAVES & STEMS Short, slim stems without any leaves or thorns.

SIZE & IMPACT Small-sized flowers – no more than 2.5cm (1in) wide.

PERFECT FOR … Buttonholes and smaller bouquets. Or use to create small, intimate displays.

ROSE HIPS

HIPS Glossy, deep red, oval hips – the natural fruit of a rose, left behind after the petals have fallen away.

LEAVES & STEMS Short fine, slightly downy stems, with a few small, downy leaves.

SIZE & IMPACT Fine, branching stems that bear several hips in a variety of sizes.

PERFECT FOR … Arrangements with an autumnal or wintry theme; combining with open roses to create striking Christmas displays.

FILLER PLANTS

When you are creating a silk flower display, you often need more than just colourful flowers and foliage – this is where the filler plants come in. These are plants that bear interesting and unusual buds, flowers, seedheads or other features. Filler plants – such as bare twigs, spiky grasses or fruiting stems – will help you add different textures and shapes to your arrangements.

HOLLYHOCK BUDS

FLOWERS Unopened buds are the key feature on this silk flower. The green, egg-shaped buds vary in size.
LEAVES & STEMS Thick, upright stems with multiple branches that bear the flower buds. Large, pale green, slightly lobed leaves.
SIZE & IMPACT Tall stems bear a profusion of distinctive buds, 1–2.5cm (¼–1in) in length.
PERFECT FOR … Adding height to a display and a touch of light green without the density of a stem of foliage.

CAT'S TAIL GRASS

FLOWERS Although they don't look like it, these fluffy spikes are the flowerheads of the cat's tail grass.
LEAVES & STEMS Very thick, flexible stems; spiky grass leaves.
SIZE & IMPACT Small flowerheads, up to 5cm (2in) long, with a pale, fluffy appearance.
PERFECT FOR … Displays that mix various grasses with cottage-garden-style flowers; arrangements that combine several types of foliage plant.

MEADOW CAT'S TAIL

FLOWERS Long, fluffy flowerheads that taper to a point; the green stem is visible through the fine, fluffy white flowers.
LEAVES & STEMS Short, pliable stems with slender, thin leaves, striped with red and with a darker green central rib running through it.
SIZE & IMPACT Distinctive, soft-looking flower spikes, up to 12.5cm (5in) long, with a floppy habit.
PERFECT FOR … Displays that combine different grasses with softly coloured, delicate flowers.

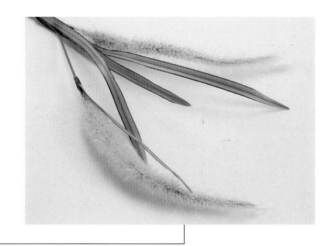

HEBE

FLOWERS Long, tapering flowerheads bearing masses of individual green flower buds. The flower spikes are flexible.

LEAVES & STEMS Thick, erect stems with a few spear-like leaves held just below the flower spikes.

SIZE & IMPACT Tall stems with unusual flowerheads, measuring up to 18cm (7in) long. The flower spikes can be bent in to various shapes.

PERFECT FOR … Complementing showy flowers with wide, open blooms in order to add height and vertical shaping.

IVY FLOWERS

FLOWERS Ivy blooms are unusual and look more like fruit than flowers; they come in faded shades of green and purple or in an off-white.

LEAVES & STEMS Short stems with few small leaves.

SIZE & IMPACT Stems bear several flowerheads, up to 5cm (2in) across; the unusual shape and colour is striking.

PERFECT FOR … Seasonal wreaths or bouquets, and where you wish to add spherical shapes in amongst colourful flowers and contrasting foliage.

LAVENDER STEMS

FLOWERS Insignificant, small flowers with a few mauve petals form a spike at the top of the stem.

LEAVES & STEMS Long, very thin, grey-green stems with bushy sprigs of grey-green, needle-like leaves.

SIZE & IMPACT Tall stems with short flower spikes, about 2.5cm (1in) long; useful feathery leaves.

PERFECT FOR … Adding height to a display but not bulk or weight; the small flowers and feathery leaves add a delicate shape to an arrangement.

DRIED PEONY BUDS

FLOWERS The dried form of peony buds; a hint of deep pink petals is visible at the tip of the green buds.

LEAVES & STEMS Thick, branching stems with a few spear-like leaves.

SIZE & IMPACT Long or mid-length stems with distinctive flower buds, about 2.5cm (1in) long.

PERFECT FOR … Displays in which you need to add more green but don't want to add more leaves; anywhere that needs a strongly shaped filler plant.

PUSSY WILLOW WITH LEAVES

FLOWERS Numerous fluffy green catkins that are borne close to the stem.

LEAVES & STEMS Twiggy stems with several branches; small light-green, spear-like leaves are spaced evenly along the branches.

SIZE & IMPACT The catkins are small – about 1cm (½in) long – but they make distinctive shapes along the stem.

PERFECT FOR … Adding to displays where strong, vertical lines are needed to break up the background.

PUSSY WILLOW STEM

FLOWERS Soft, grey, fluffy catkins form the flowers of the willow tree.

LEAVES & STEMS Stiff, erect stems without leaves; the catkins are borne tightly against the stem.

SIZE & IMPACT Stems are long and without any protruding branches. The catkins are plentiful and run along the stem.

PERFECT FOR … Adding height, structure and a depth of colour to an arrangement; add several to a display and fan them out to create a strong, even shape.

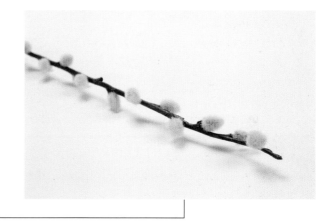

ARTICHOKE BUD

FLOWERS The closed bud of the globe artichoke is made up of light green scales, tinged with red.

LEAVES & STEMS Thick, upright stems with glossy, green, oval leaves positioned just below the bud.

SIZE & IMPACT Long, greeny-brown stems with strongly shaped leaves and a large bud formation at the tip.

PERFECT FOR … Complementing large, single blooms, such as hydrangeas, viburnum, agapanthus and amaryllis to create a bold display.

ARTICHOKE

FLOWERS The flower of a globe artichoke is made up of thick green, tooth-tipped scales rather than petals.

LEAVES & STEMS Strong, thick stem with no leaves; the flower head is borne at the end of the stem.

SIZE & IMPACT These very large flowers measure 15–20cm (8–10in) across.

PERFECT FOR … Winter displays using dark flowers. For an architectural display, arrange at various heights to form a neat pyramid shape; or use singly in a small planter.

COW PARSLEY STEM

FLOWERS Small-sized flowerheads, made up of clusters of tiny white flowers.

LEAVES & STEMS Ridged upright stems, with slender branches at the very top that bear the flowerheads and lobed leaves.

SIZE & IMPACT Feathery leaves and small flower clusters – up to 5cm (2in) across – at the top of long stems.

PERFECT FOR … Open, loose displays with plenty of other lacy flowers and greenery.

BEECH TWIGS

FLOWERS Flowerless stems.

LEAVES & STEMS Many fine and delicate branches emerging from one main stem. Small nodules along the stem but no leaves.

SIZE & IMPACT Each reddy-brown stem features lots of slightly curled, thin twigs with slender tips.

PERFECT FOR … Adding fine, delicate and twisting lines to a display. Use with large, single flowers, such as lilies or amaryllis, to give more texture.

BIRCH TWIGS

FLOWERS Flowerless stems.

LEAVES & STEMS Stems with long, slender, branches that are fine and very thin at the tip. Pale green, round leaves are borne on fine white stems.

SIZE & IMPACT Each stem features many thin, dark-brown branches; the small, bright leaves seem to shimmer on the stem.

PERFECT FOR … Mixing with strongly shaped flowers, such as roses and peonies, to create a light and feathery outline.

BUDDING TWIGS

FLOWERS Flowerless stems.

LEAVES & STEMS Many fine, twiggy stems with a few short branches are connected together to form a stretchy lattice. They bear a few small leaves.

SIZE & IMPACT The mass of criss-crossing stems can be stretched open, bundled up tightly or rolled up within a vase.

PERFECT FOR … Creating a holding structure in to which other flowers can be arranged. The lattice can be cut up and the twigs used separately.

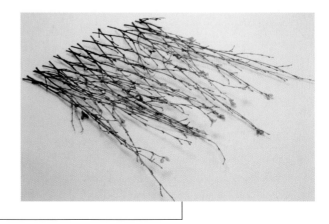

GREENERY

Although you can create fantastic displays using flowers alone, more often than not you will need some greenery to act as a foil to the colour of the blooms. Many silk flowers come with leaves attached and so you may not have to add any extra foliage, but there are often times when you do need more greenery and this is when individual sprays of silk foliage are invaluable.

CAMELLIA FOLIAGE

FLOWERS Flowerless stems.
LEAVES & STEMS Tall, slightly knobbly, upright stems, with several branches. The dark- and mid-green leaves are oval and pointed at the tips. The edges are slightly serrated.
SIZE & IMPACT Long stems with abundant glossy leaves, 5–7.5cm (2–3in) long.
PERFECT FOR ... Creating imposing backgrounds. Ideal for dividing in to smaller sections.

UMBRELLA PAPYRUS

FLOWERS Flowerless stems.
LEAVES & STEMS Long, straight stems with the grass-like leaves emerging at the tip. The leaves fan outwards in a circular shape, hence the name.
SIZE & IMPACT Tall stems with all the interest focused at the tip. The leaf-clump is up to 30cm (12in) across.
PERFECT FOR ... Combining with large, exotic blooms for a dramatic arrangement.

MEADOW GRASS CLUMP

FLOWERS One or two blooms made up of many tiny purple flowers.
LEAVES & STEMS Short stems from which numerous fine blades of grass emerge.
SIZE & IMPACT A thick clump of grass leaves, each measuring up to 30cm (12in) in length.
PERFECT FOR ... Arrangements that combine wild flowers or cottage-garden blooms with mixed grasses. Also ideal for any informal display that needs the addition of fine areas of foliage.

MEADOW GRASS LEAVES

FLOWERS Flowerless stems.

LEAVES & STEMS Very thin, short stems, bearing eight to ten single blades of grass in varying shades of green.

SIZE & IMPACT The fine blades of grass are 25–30cm (10–12in) long and fan open slightly from the stem.

PERFECT FOR … Any display in which you need to add a few grassy leaves; combine with delicate flowers, such as love-in-a-mist and poppies, to create the mood of a natural meadow.

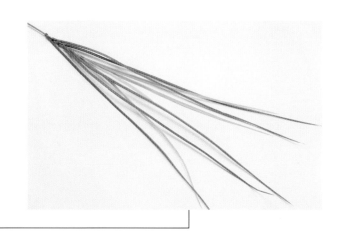

SKIMMIA

FLOWERS Clusters of tiny, greeny-brown flowers.

LEAVES & STEMS Tall, thin stems with a few branches at the very top. The long oval leaves are finished with a slightly downy sheen.

SIZE & IMPACT The leaves are 5–7.5cm (2–3in) long; the flowerheads are up to 5cm (2in) across.

PERFECT FOR … Achieving a variety of green shades with only one plant – skimmia's mix of greenish flowers and foliage offers a unique combination.

HOPS

FLOWERS Pale green flowers – the hops – that look like inverted pine cones.

LEAVES & STEMS Long, branching stems – known as bines – with twining tips. Abundant lobed and oval leaves.

SIZE & IMPACT The leaves are up to 7.5cm (3in) across. The hops, although only 2.5cm (1in) long, are distinctive due to their pale colour and interesting layered shape.

PERFECT FOR … Any display for which you require a foliage plant that gently droops or falls over the edge of a vase, or mingles closely with other plants.

MAPLE LEAVES

FLOWERS Flowerless stems.

LEAVES & STEMS Tall, slightly bending, twiggy
stems bearing a mass of hand-shaped leaves in
autumnal shades of mottled green, yellow and red.

SIZE & IMPACT Long stems with lots of leaves,
each up to 7.5cm (3in) across.

PERFECT FOR ... Using in winter- and autumn-
themed displays; ideal as a background for
dark-coloured and strongly shaped flowers,
such as hydrangeas.

SAGE

FLOWERS Flowerless stems.

LEAVES & STEMS Short, thin, grey stems bear
numerous short, strap-like grey-green leaves with
distinctive toothed edges.

SIZE & IMPACT Short stems with a multitude of
distinctive leaves, up to 7.5cm (3in) long.

PERFECT FOR ... Combining with other grey-green
foliage plants and using as a contrasting foil to
blue and purple flowers.

ROSEMARY

FLOWERS Flowerless stems.

LEAVES & STEMS Thin, short, branching stems that
bear grey-green, needle-like leaves along the length.

SIZE & IMPACT Leaves vary in size – the longest are
about 2cm (¾in) – and give stems a feathery look.

PERFECT FOR ... Mixed arrangements, combined
with other grey-green leaves; include rosemary
when you want to break up the density of the green
foliage in a display.

BAMBOO LEAVES

FLOWERS Flowerless stems.

LEAVES & STEMS Slim stems with plenty of knobbly joints. Glossy, sword-like leaves with a faint rusty tinge at the tip.

SIZE & IMPACT Tall stems with an interesting outline; the leaves are up to 7.5cm (3in) long.

PERFECT FOR ... Grand, architectural displays where unusual and abundant foliage is needed. Combine with exotic flowers, such as lilies.

EUCALYPTUS

FLOWERS A few tiny clusters of insignificant, grey-green flower buds.

LEAVES & STEMS Thin stems with long, spear-like leaves with a grey-green tinge and slightly edged with rust red.

SIZE & IMPACT Short to medium-length stems with long leaves, up to 10cm (4in) in length.

PERFECT FOR ... Creating an interesting background of foliage; combine with a variety of different types of foliage for a variety in shades of green.

HONEYSUCKLE

FLOWERS A few clusters of cream or pale orange, trumpet-shaped flowers, borne at the base of branches.

LEAVES & STEMS Very long, flexible stems with several long branches bearing pairs of oval leaves. Only one or two stems bear flowers.

SIZE & IMPACT Very tall stems with smallish leaves (no more than 2.5cm (1in) long) borne along most of the length.

PERFECT FOR ... Adding height and width to a display. Ideal for dividing in to several smaller sections.

MOTH ORCHID LEAVES

FLOWERS No flowers attached.

LEAVES & STEMS Up to six, very thick and wide, interlocking leaves are held on a short stem; a few aerial roots are attached.

SIZE & IMPACT The largest of the leaves is about 25cm (10in) long and 10cm (4in) wide; the leaves fan outwards.

PERFECT FOR … Using with moth orchid flowers or in any display in which you need thick, exotic-looking leaves that will sit just on top of the container.

CYMBIDIUM ORCHID LEAVES

FLOWERS No flowers attached.

LEAVES & STEMS No stem to speak of: the leaves are bound together at the base, with a few aerial roots. The long, sword-like leaves are folded back slightly along the central rib.

SIZE & IMPACT About eight leaves to a clump, up to 2.5cm (1in) wide and 30–35cm (12–14in) long.

PERFECT FOR … Use with cymbidium orchids and in any display requiring tall and slender, exotic leaves.

ASPIDISTRA LEAVES

FLOWERS No flowers attached.

LEAVES & STEMS A slim stem bears a single, large leaf with several vertical ribs. Various shades of green are found within one leaf.

SIZE & IMPACT The leaves are up to 35cm (14in) long and 12.5cm (5in) wide. Each leaf is flexible.

PERFECT FOR … Lining glass vases in order to conceal Oasis foam support. Or use in displays that combine exotic blooms, such as calla lilies and amaryllis.

CHAPTER 2

Silk flower essentials

To arrange silk flowers to the maximum effect, you will need a few simple tools and accessories. This chapter offers an invaluable guide to the different materials and techniques used for creating stunning, successful, professional-looking displays.

CONTAINERS

When it comes to picking a container for your silk flower display, the choice
of what to use is more-or-less limitless. Since you don't necessarily need to use
a watertight vase, your range of options is truly infinite.

When you're creating an arrangement of silk flowers, you need to start with a suitable container. Although you can use almost anything for a silk flower display, you should always consider whether the vase will complement the flowers you've chosen. Make sure the colour or design of the container does not clash with the colours of the flowers you're going to use. Pick a pot that's the right shape for the arrangement you are planning; a shallow container, for example, won't work with an upright display. And make sure that the container is the correct scale and proportion for your flowers; a short and wide vase will not be the right choice for a tall and thin display. You may also like to consider whether your chosen container will match its intended setting: if, for example, you wish to create a display for a formal, elegant room, then a rustic tin container may not look quite right.

In most silk flower arrangements, the stems of the plants are held in place by a support medium; this might be Oasis foam (see page 47) or acrylic water (see page 49). You can, of course, simply arrange your flowers in your chosen container without any support; though bear in mind that the container needs to be sturdy enough for your arrangement and that if you move the container, the silk flowers will move around and alter the appearance of the overall display.

If you are using Oasis, then your chosen container needs to be big enough to accommodate the foam. Fortunately, you can cut Oasis into pieces to get the perfect fit (see page 48). Acrylic water is a clear resin that looks like water, but which sets solid to hold your flower display in place. It's used when you want to create a display in a glass vase, where the Oasis foam would show through the container.

*For a simple arrangement
of cottage-garden plants,
such as these purple
pansies, a country-style
container will be ideal.*

CERAMIC CONTAINERS

Traditional ceramic vases and bowls are all ideal for silk flower arrangements. If you are creating a large and impressive display, then a decorative glazed china bowl is perfect – it will have just the right impact and be sturdy enough to support both flowers and foliage. Wide or shallow bowls can be very tricky to use with fresh flowers because the blooms can flop forwards and simply fall out. But with silk flowers, you will not have this problem: simply fill the container with Oasis foam and glue in place (see page 47). Then position your silk flowers as necessary for a secure and stunning display.

BASKETS

If you use a closely woven basket, then simply pack it with Oasis first – the foam should not be visible through the weave. But if your basket is fairly open, then line it with artificial moss or leaves before adding the Oasis to conceal the foam. Alternatively, insert another container inside the basket and arrange the Oasis and flowers within that.

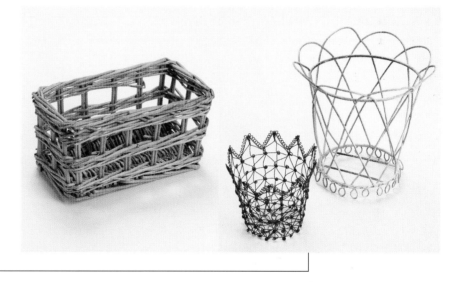

WOODEN CONTAINERS

If you wanted to use a wooden container to arrange fresh flowers, then you would need to find a suitable liner with which to make it watertight. But with silk flowers, this will not be necessary: all you have to do is secure some Oasis inside the container before adding the flowers. Wooden containers also offer a great deal of decorative scope: an old wine box, complete with label, would make a charming informal holder for country flowers and grasses. You could also decorate a wooden container yourself: paint on stencilled designs or apply découpage for some interesting effects.

CLAY POTS

Although containers made from terracotta – or any other unglazed clay – are porous, you can still use them with silk flowers to mimic the 'potted-up' appearance of real flowers. Simple flowerpots can look charming, especially when used with cottage-garden flowers and plants – such as pansies and miniature daffodils. But larger flowerpots and terracotta planters can look just as attractive, and make ideal containers for arrangements that are to be displayed in porches, hallways and conservatories.

TIN CONTAINERS

A wide range of tin – and other metal – containers is available, in all sorts of shapes and sizes. Some are bare metal, and may be decorated with moulded patterns, while others are painted or enamelled. You can also redecorate tin containers yourself – see below.

PLASTIC CONTAINERS

Occasionally, you may be creating a silk flower display where the container is completely covered by the flowers and foliage placed within it, or where the container is concealed within another pot. In this instance, plastic or acrylic containers, ideally with an edge or lip, are ideal. Clear plastic is particularly useful because you are less likely to see it through the arrangement. Plastic food containers may be kept for this purpose, and are an economic option if creating many small displays.

Sylvia says ...

If you want to match a container to your décor, then it's often quite an easy matter to adapt it with paint. Tin containers are ideal for this. Start by brushing the tin with a wire brush to remove any dirt or debris, and then rub lightly all over with some fine-grade steel wool – it's better to paint on a slightly matte surface. Mask off any areas of the container that you don't want to paint, and then coat with a suitable metal primer. When that's dry, paint with the colour of your choice. You can use a specialist paint for metal, but household emulsion should be fine if you've primed the surface first.

PLANT SUPPORTS

When you've spent time putting together the perfect silk flower arrangement,
you want your creation to look good for as long as possible. Use the right support to
hold your silk flowers in place and your display will last for as long as you want.

The most common support medium used in artificial flower arrangements is dry floral foam, also often known by its trademark name, Oasis. Floral foam has been around since the 1950s and was first developed for use with fresh flower arrangements. The foam used with silk flowers is, as its name suggests, intended to be used dry – in fact it also is sometimes known as Sahara floral foam. The Oasis foam used with fresh flowers differs from dry floral foam in that it is designed to absorb water.

Oasis foam is sold in blocks, in a wide range of shapes and sizes: you'll find various squares and rectangles, cylindrical shapes, cones and even spheres. You can also buy foam that is made specifically for creating certain types of display – such as bouquets, wreaths and garlands. Oasis foam is not expensive and is usually sold in multiple packs. Even if you cannot find a foam block to exactly fit your chosen container, Oasis is easy to cut into shape.

When you use Oasis it's best to secure it to the container before you begin your arrangement. You can use special pot tape or Oasis floral adhesive – the latter is also useful for holding plant stems in place in the Oasis. A hot-glue gun is also handy. If you don't want to stick the foam to your chosen pot, then you could consider finding a plastic pot that fits in your container and then stick the foam in that; the plastic pot will need to fit very snugly.

Oasis foam isn't particularly attractive, so once you've filled your container with it, you will want to conceal it from view, especially if your finished display is not one that will cover the top of the container. The best way to do this is to lay artificial moss over the top. This can be secured with bent wire pins or with glue. The stems of your silk flowers can be simply pressed into the Oasis foam through the moss.

*Although it is an incredibly useful supporting medium,
Oasis foam is not particularly attractive. So if you
want to use it in a glass bowl or vase, you may wish
to conceal it in some way. One way of doing this is to
slip larger artificial leaves down the side of the vase, in
between the Oasis foam and the glass.*

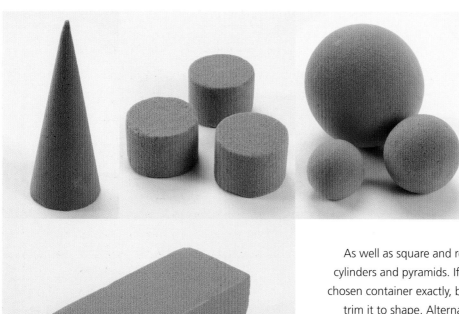

TYPES OF OASIS

As well as square and rectangular blocks, Oasis comes in cylinders and pyramids. If you don't find a block to fit your chosen container exactly, buy one that is too large and then trim it to shape. Alternatively, you can use a block that is smaller, and then cut pieces from another block to fill in the gaps. Spherical Oasis is useful since you can cut the blocks into a variety of shapes. If you trim off a small section at the bottom, then the Oasis will be able to stand flat. Or you can cut a sphere in half to make a hemisphere; ideal for wide, branching displays, such as table centrepieces.

CUTTING OASIS

It is very easy to cut blocks of Oasis into new shapes or to fit a specific container. All you need is a sharp cook's knife – one with a serrated blade is ideal. As you cut into the Oasis you will find that minute granules of foam come off onto your hands and onto the work surface. If you find the granules irritate your skin, wear latex gloves for this job. Also, cut the Oasis outside or in a well-ventilated room to avoid breathing in the granules. Wear a face mask if you are cutting up a lot of foam.

MOSS

Artificial moss is used to cover the top of the Oasis in your container. It can also be used to line a container – such as a basket or glass vase – where you want to conceal the sides of the Oasis. Secure the moss to the foam with bent wire pins or with Oasis adhesive.

ACRYLIC WATER

Acrylic water acts both as a support for your silk flowers and as artificial water. It is perfect, therefore, for tall glass vases where Oasis cannot be used. Acrylic water is sometimes sold under the name of 'floral setting resin' or 'clear epoxy resin'.

Acrylic water is made by mixing together two chemical substances. It is then poured into the chosen container and the flowers are arranged in the mixture before it sets. Once the arrangement is completely finished, it is put aside for the resin to set solid; this can take up to 48 hours. For additional support at the base of the container, place glass marbles in the bottom of the vase first, then pour in the resin before arranging the flowers.

Great care needs to be taken when using acrylic water. Follow the manufacturer's instructions to the letter, wear latex or rubber gloves, and work in a well-ventilated area. Always read the cautionary notices that come with the resin and ensure that you have everything to hand before you start working. Never dispose of acrylic-water products down the drain or pour the unwanted mixture into the sink – it will set solid and block your drainage system. If you make up more acrylic water than you need, pour the leftovers into an old plastic container and leave to set. You can then dispose of the plastic container and the set resin together.

> ### Sylvia says ...
>
> *To make sure you don't make up more acrylic water than you need, you should work out the amount required before you start. Take your chosen vase and pour in tap water up to the level you will need. Then pour this into a measuring jug and make a note of the amount of water you have. Use this measurement when you mix up the acrylic water. Remember to clean and dry your chosen vase thoroughly. Once the acrylic water has been used and has hardened, it will be impossible to clean off any dirt or water marks on the inside of the vase.*

USING ACRYLIC WATER

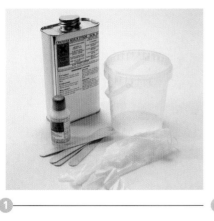

1

To create acrylic water, you need to mix two separate substances. You will need a plastic container, marked with liquid measurements, or a measuring jug. You will also need something to stir the two substances – a wooden spatula is ideal. Suppliers of acrylic water often also sell equipment with which to mix the chemicals. You will also need latex or rubber gloves to protect your hands.

2

Pour the required amount of resin into your plastic container and then add the accelerant. Stir the two together gently, taking care not the splash the liquid ingredients.

3

Pour the mixture into your chosen vase or bowl. Pour it very slowly and in a steady stream to avoid splashing the acrylic water up on to the sides of the container. Once the vase is filled, carefully check the sides for splashes and wipe these off with a soft, clean cloth. Once hardened, these spots of acrylic water will be impossible to remove from the surface of the vase.

Oasis and acrylic water are invaluable when it comes to supporting the stems of silk flowers and holding your arrangement in place, but there are other pieces of equipment you may need that offer different kinds of support to your silk flowers and foliage.

Some silk flowers have soft, pliable stems that can bend or flop in one direction. Generally speaking, you will want to exploit these characteristics in your arrangements, but occasionally you may want to prevent a flowerhead drooping too far. In this instance, you can use ordinary plant supports – the kind of plant stakes used for real house plants.

Sometimes you need to bind silk flowers together – or to a plant support – and so you need some kind of tie.

Old-fashioned raffia is a good option; it is cheap and, if the tie is visible, it looks charming in a rustic or country-style arrangement. Florists' tape is also invaluable. It is very slightly tacky, so that when you wrap it around flower stems the ends stick to each other. The tape is coloured green and so does not need to be completely concealed, but it is not particularly decorative and best reserved for those instances when it will be hidden among the flowers or inside a vase.

Equally useful are ordinary green or brown garden twine and florists' wire. As with raffia, the twine can be used to simply wrap and tie around a bunch of flowers; florists' wire needs to be bent around the stems and the ends twisted together to secure.

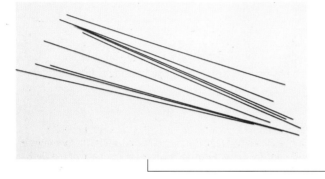

PLANT STAKES

The type of stake or cane used to support house plants can also be used in silk flower arrangements. Push them into the Oasis foam next to the stem you want to support and use raffia or florists' wire to secure the stem to the stake, much as you would in the garden.

TIES

Low-tack florists' tape is a useful item for your silk flower tool box. It can be wrapped around flower stems to hold them together in a bunch, or it can be used to attach one piece of a stem to another – for example, when repairing a flower or extending its stem (see page 124). Although the tape is usually green, it may not match the stems of your flowers to make an invisible mend. Florists' tape is also useful as a temporary support for flowers when you are arranging stems in acrylic water (see page 110).

Florists' wire is sold either covered or uncovered – the covered variety is usually encased in green plastic. The wire can be wound around the stems, then twisted together to secure. You will need to use pliers or wire cutters to trim the ends. If you use florists' wire to bind flowers in a bouquet, remember to wrap ribbon around the wire to cover the ends.

Raffia and garden twine are both simple ways to tie together silk flowers and are well worth keeping to hand. The only thing you need to remember when using these is to wrap them very tightly around the stems and tie the finishing knot securely so that it does not unravel.

WORKING WITH SILK FLOWERS

To create the perfect silk flower display, you may have to manipulate the silk flowers into a new position. This may be simply a case of bending or twisting the plants, but it might also mean cutting flowers or foliage down to size, or joining elements to create new design opportunities.

When you are using silk flowers, sometimes the stems and the blooms do not go quite where you want them to and you may have to twist and turn the stems in the Oasis or the vase in order to get their position just right. Some flowers have wired stems and so it is very easy to bend these into position. And even the unwired flowers often have very flexible stems that can be bent or reshaped.

When you unwrap new silk flowers, or when you take older flowers out of storage, you may find that the leaves and flowers are a little bent out of shape or alignment. It is a good idea, therefore, to gently tease the flowers and leaves back into shape. Sometimes, all you need to do is take hold of the stem and gently shake the flowerhead so that the petals and stamens fall back into place.

Another way to freshen up silk flowers is to steam them: hold the flower by the end of the stem to avoid scalding yourself and position the petals over the spout of a steaming kettle for a few seconds. Remove from the heat and gently tweak the petals and leaves into position with your fingertips.

Sometimes, silk flowers are not quite the right length for your chosen design. More often that not, they are too long and you need to either shorten the stems or trim off smaller branches. This is easily done with a pair of wire cutters: they must be strong and sharp enough to cut through wire-filled stems or branches. Smaller stems and unwired stems can be cut with kitchen scissors. Do not throw away excess stems or branches: use them to extend shorter stems or to repair broken flowers (see page 124).

Many flowers feature many smaller branches, or come with several stems; viburnum, for example, comes in stems that feature many branches and multiple flowerheads. You may need to trim off some of the branches to make the stem fit your display, or you may want to divide it up to get more out of the one piece. All you need to do is use scissors or cutters to remove the excess branches; do this close to the main stem. Some silk flowers come with buds or seedheads attached and you may want to use these separately – either in the same display or a different arrangement. Again, it's a simple matter to cut these off.

There are many arrangements where you will not require the full length of a silk flower stem. If you are creating a wreath, for example, you will want the flowerheads to lie close to the surface of the Oasis foam ring. You will, therefore, have to cut the stems short so that they do not go all the way through the Oasis.

You may also want to remove the leaves from a flower stem and set aside for a later project or use them in a different position. Fortunately, most flowers come with abundant foliage. You can also buy large branches of different kinds of foliage and you will find that you can often cut these into smaller sections to get the most out of one stem.

Just as you may want to cut away parts of a flower, you may also want to add additional elements. It could be that you need to repair a silk flower – petals do fall off – but you may also want to augment a silk bloom by adding extra petals, stamens or additional leaves. The best way to do this is to use a hot-glue gun. The adhesive that you can apply with the gun is very strong, and the glue-gun method of application means that you can be extremely accurate with the nozzle. The glue gun can also be useful to secure drooping stems to the edge of a vase: just put a drop of glue on the edge of the vase where it will not be seen and then press the stem on to the glue. Always protect your work surface and wear protective gloves when using a hot-glue gun. Work in a well-ventilated area or outside to minimize the effect of the glue fumes.

CUTTING

Cutting through silk flower stems, even wired ones, is easy if you have a decent pair of cutters. Ordinary wire cutters should do the job, though you may want to buy those designed specifically for silk flowers. Simply put the stem in between the pincers, at the point where you want to cut, and squeeze the handles gently together.

Sylvia says ...

Because I create silk flower arrangements, I'm constantly cutting into the stems of the flowers. So to make my life a little bit easier, I invested in a specialist cutting tool called an Easy Cutter. You place the flower stem under a blade and then lower the blade with a lever; the action is much easier on the hands when you are cutting as many stems as I do!

DIVIDING SILK FLOWERS

Many silk flowers are made up of smaller branches or stems, attached to one main stem. This means that you can often divide up one stem and get several smaller sections. Pansies, for example, come in a clump and bear lots of smaller flowering stems and leaves. You can use scissors (or cutters) to trim the clump into smaller sections and then combine these with other silk flowers.

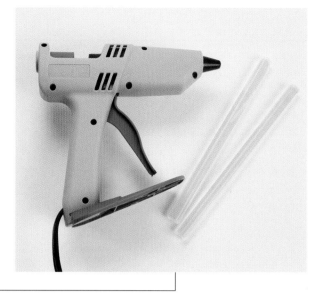

HOT-GLUE GUN

A hot-glue gun works by electrically heating solid cold glue until liquid, then releasing drops of the hot adhesive through a nozzle. The hot glue is more effective as an adhesive than standard cold glues and provides more control on application. The glue for the gun is sold in self-contained sticks or cylinders: the stick is inserted into the gun, the gun is plugged in, then turned on to heat. Squeezing the trigger releases a spot of glue from the nozzle.

STEAMING

To refresh silk flowers that have been crushed or that have folded petals, simply bring a kettle to the boil and hold the flowerhead over the steam for a few seconds. Draw the flower away from the steam and use your fingertips to gently smooth out any folds or creases, and to fluff open flowerheads that are too tightly packed together. The same trick works with foliage too.

Sylvia says ...

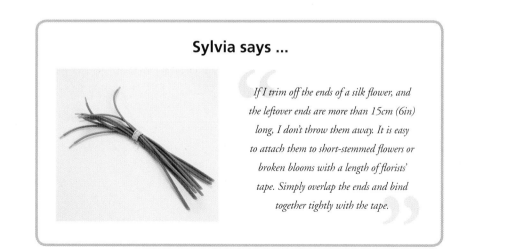

If I trim off the ends of a silk flower, and the leftover ends are more than 15cm (6in) long, I don't throw them away. It is easy to attach them to short-stemmed flowers or broken blooms with a length of florists' tape. Simply overlap the ends and bind together tightly with the tape.

CHAPTER 3

Silk flowers for the home

Bringing silk flowers in to your home will both enhance and revitalize your décor. Displays can be as simple or as elaborate as you wish because there's a perfect style for everyone, and you can enjoy the beautiful blooms forever!

HEART OF THE HOME

The deep dusky hues of burgundy hydrangeas form a perfect contrast to the
light green shades of lady's mantle, viburnum and dill flowers in this stunning arrangement.
The sculptural heads of artichokes give the display structure and shape. Such pleasing
combinations are sure to bring cheer to any hearth or home.

You will need

- large oval ceramic container, about 20cm (8in) tall, 50cm (20in) wide and 15cm (6in) deep
- Oasis foam
- Oasis adhesive
- moss
- bent wire pins (optional)
- 10 stems of camellia foliage
- 1 leafless beech twig
- 1 euonymus stem
- 6 stems of lady's mantle
- 1 giant dill flowerhead
- 2 light green viburnum stems
- 4 dusky burgundy hydrangeas
- 1 large artichoke
- 4 small artichokes

1 Cut your Oasis foam to fit your container (if necessary) and then secure it in place with adhesive. Arrange moss over the top of the Oasis. You can use the adhesive to secure the moss, or insert some bent wire pins to hold it down. Take four stems of camellia foliage and push them in to the Oasis towards the back of the container.

2 Add the remaining camellia foliage, pushing more stems in towards the back of the container. Ensure that you have a stem on either side that hangs down over the edge of the container – this will help give the arrangement width. Carefully insert a couple of stems closer to the front of the container and let these fall forwards slightly.

Design ideas

This display works by contrasting light-coloured flowers – lady's mantle, dill and viburnum – with large, densely coloured flowers – hydrangeas and artichokes. You can use this principle to adapt the arrangement: swap the viburnum for cow parsley or Queen Anne's lace, for example; and use purple alliums and mauve peonies instead of the hydrangeas and artichokes.

3 Take the beech twig and push it in to the Oasis towards the centre-back of the container. Take the euonymus stem and cut it in to three or four smaller sections. Push these in to the Oasis at the centre of the arrangement, in between the camellia stems.

4 Take three stems of lady's mantle and push them in to the Oasis towards the back of the arrangement, but in front of the camellia foliage you put in place at step 1. Space them evenly across the width of the display. Take the remaining lady's mantle and push the stems in to the Oasis towards the front. Push these stems in further so that they are at a lower level than the lady's mantle towards the back.

5

Push the giant dill flowerhead in to the Oasis at the centre of the display so that is between the two rows of lady's mantle inserted in step 4. Place a viburnum stem on either side of the dill flowerhead, positioned so that it is between the two rows of lady's mantle.

6

Take two of the hydrangeas and insert one on the far left of the display, and one on the far right, angling the stems as you push them in to the Oasis so that the flowers point outwards at each side. Try to angle each one so that the flowers face forwards slightly. Take another hydrangea and insert it at the centre of the display, angling the stem as you push it in to the Oasis so that the flower droops forwards over the edge of the container. Insert the last hydrangea at the back of the container, positioned behind the dill flowerhead.

7

Take the large artichoke and insert the stem at the centre of the display, just behind the central hydrangea. Take two of the smaller artichoke heads and insert one on the left and one on the right, positioning them in front of the hydrangeas at the side of the arrangement. Take the remaining two artichokes and position these just behind the hydrangeas at the side.

POPPIES AND PINCUSHIONS

This delicate mixture of pinks and mauves is as pretty as a picture. The wide open blooms of the poppies, with their papery petals, contrast with the tightly packed flowerheads of the pincushions.

You will need

- cylindrical glass vase, about 15cm (6in) tall and 20cm (8in) in diameter
- Oasis foam
- Oasis adhesive
- moss
- bent wire pins (optional)
- 8–10 hydrangea leaves
- 4–5 clumps of meadow grass
- 10 long lavender stems
- 15 short lavender stems
- 3 poppy buds
- 5–6 white pincushions (scabious)
- 5–6 pink pincushions (scabious)
- 4 stems of blush-pink poppies
- 5 stems of dark pink poppies

Sylvia says ...

Each of the silk poppies I use in my displays usually comes with two stems, one with an open flower attached, one with a bud. Sometimes I only want to use the open flowers and so I cut off the stem with the bud. But I don't throw these away since they make fantastic fillers – in this arrangement I've used several buds to add interest.

1 Cut your Oasis to fit your container (if necessary) and then secure it in place with glue. Make sure there is a gap between the Oasis and the vase around the sides. Arrange moss over the top of the Oasis. You can use the adhesive to secure the moss, or insert some bent wire pins to hold it down. Slip the hydrangea leaves in between the Oasis and the sides of the vase, making sure the leaves overlap and conceal the Oasis.

2 Take the clumps of meadow grass and push them through the moss in to the Oasis. Position the clumps so that you have one or two at the back of the vase, with the remaining grass on either side and angled slightly forwards.

3 Take three or four of the long lavender stems and arrange them at the sides of the vase, so that they fall forwards and outwards. Then arrange the remaining long lavender stems at the centre of the display, so that the flowerheads stand taller than the meadow grass. Use the short lavender stems to fill in around the sides of the display, angling the stems so that they point outwards.

4 Insert two of the poppy buds in the front of the display. Push the stems well down in to the Oasis and angle them so that they flop down over the front of the vase. Add the remaining poppy bud towards the back of the arrangement, inserting the stem at a slight angle. Don't push the third stem in too far – the poppy bud should remain tall.

5

Add one white pincushion stem at the back of the display so that it stands tall and straight, roughly in the centre. Insert one white pincushion at either side of the vase, so that they flop forwards and the flowers are angled slightly towards the front. Add the remaining white pincushions towards the back of the display so that they fan outwards. Don't push the stems in too far – keep the flowers tall.

6

Take three or four of the pink pincushions and use to fill in the centre of the display; angle the flowerheads so that they face forwards and push the stems in so that the flowers are slightly lower than the rest of the display. Add the remaining pink pincushions, using them to fill in around the back of the display. Insert the stems at an angle and push them in so that the flowers are at a lower level than the white pincushions.

7

Take the three blush-pink poppies and use to fill in at the centre of the display. Keep them tall, and angle the stems slightly so that the flowers fall outwards or forwards.

8

Take one dark pink poppy and add it at the centre-front of the display; push the stem well in so that the flower is surrounded by the pink pincushions. Add the remaining dark pink poppies around the back of the display, inserting them between the blush-pink poppies and angling the stems so that the flowers fall slightly outwards or forwards. Keep these dark pink poppies the same height as the blush pink ones.

THE SPRING COLLECTION

For a real breath of fresh air, why not bring the clean, bright blooms of spring in to your home? The cool, white flowers of narcissi, hyacinth and miniature alliums are arranged in individual pots to create a simple, yet effective display.

You will need

- 3 identical tin pots, about 15cm (6in) tall and 10cm (5in) in diameter
- Oasis foam
- Oasis adhesive
- moss
- bent wire pins (optional)
- 6 miniature alliums, plus leaves
- 2 narcissi buds, plus leaves
- 2 hyacinth stems
- 4 narcissi stems, plus leaves

Sylvia says ...

I've chosen white flowers for this arrangement but you could try some other colourways. Alliums come in purple or white; hyacinths in deep blue, pink or white; and narcissi in shades of yellow or white. You could, therefore, have each flower in a different colour and mix up the spring shades. You could also try other spring flowering bulbs, such as crocus or grape hyacinth.

1 Take your first tin pot and cut your Oasis foam to fit (if necessary); secure in place with the glue. Arrange moss over the top of the Oasis and secure in place with some of the adhesive or with bent wire pins. Push the allium leaves in to the centre of the Oasis.

2 Prepare your second pot as for step 1. Take the two narcissi buds (with their attached leaves) and push these in to the centre of the Oasis foam, spacing them a small distance apart.

3 Prepare your third tin pot as in step 1. Take the narcissi leaves and one small flowering stem and push these in to the centre of the Oasis foam.

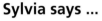

4 Take the allium flowers and press these in to the centre of the allium leaves in the first pot. Take the hyacinth stems and press these in to the centre of the second pot, just in front of the narcissi leaves. Take the remaining narcissi stems and push them in to the third pot, positioning around the clump of leaves.

LOVELY LAVENDER

Three matching pots make the ideal containers for this simple, yet pleasing, display of hand-tied lavender bunches. The feathery foliage of the lavender is a perfect foil to the tall flower spikes, and the soft, silvery, grey-green colour of the leaves contrast with the intense purple of the blooms.

You will need

- about 225 individual lavender stems

- raffia

- 3 matching containers, each about 15cm (6in) tall and 10cm (5in) in diameter

- Oasis foam (optional)

Sylvia says ...

Hand-tied bunches of any flower make ideal gifts. If you're planning on creating posies for presents, you will need to tie the bunch very neatly indeed. Try to wind the raffia or ribbon around the flower stems as evenly as you can and then finish off with a small but tidy bow. The tie needs to be tight so none of the flowers fall out. The larger your bunch, the wider your tie needs to be – not enough raffia or ribbon and the bunch will splay open. Position the tie high up the stems, just below the blooms and leaves, so that the bunch fans out slightly.

1 ————————————————————

Take your lavender and divide it in to three rough bunches of about 75 stems each. Take the first of these bunches and then divide in to five more bunches of about 15 stems each.

2 ————————————————————

Cut a length of raffia about 60cm (24in) long and use it to bind together one bunch of about 15 stems. Wrap the raffia neatly and tightly around the stems, just below the last leaves. Secure with a knot or small bow. Repeat to make up four more bunches of 15 stems each.

3 ————————————————————

If you need extra support for the flowers, place a disc of Oasis foam in the bottom of your three containers. Take your five tied bunches of lavender and arrange them in the first container. Then repeat steps 1 and 2 with the remaining lavender stems to create ten more tied bunches of lavender for the remaining two containers.

FRESH GREENS

White hydrangeas, pale green viburnum and lady's mantle are used to great effect in this
bright and airy display. The clusters of tiny blooms which make up each flowerhead give
these particular plants a light and lacy look that is well suited to a large arrangement.

You will need

- tall, cylindrical ceramic pot, with neck narrower than body, about 30cm (12in) tall, and 25cm (10in) in diameter, at widest part
- 3 large white viburnum stems
- 6 large pale green viburnum stems
- 3 large white hydrangea stems
- 6 large stems of lady's mantle

Sylvia says ...

Although this is a large and impressive arrangement, it uses a very simple colour combination of white and green. And the blooms used are very similar in their shape – all feature flowerheads made up of numerous tiny flowers. Put everything together and you have a light, cloud-like, fresh green display.

1

Take one of the white viburnum stems and place it at the centre-back of the vase. Take the other two stems and place one at the left-hand side and one at the right. This arrangement is not secured in Oasis (or any other kind of support) and so will be looser and less structured than other displays.

2

Add the pale green viburnum stems, pushing them in to the vase evenly all round the display. Mingle the pale green flowers evenly with the white viburnums. Don't push the stems in too far – you want the flowers to flop loosely out of the vase.

3

Add the white hydrangea stems; position one at the centre and one on either side. Again, don't push the stems in too far – keep the display loose and open in appearance.

4

Finally, add the lady's mantle. Insert the stems evenly all round the display, positioning the lady's mantle between the other blooms to help break up the outline of the display.

ELEGANT ORCHIDS

Add a touch of real elegance to any room with this simple, yet striking display. It takes just four stems of orchid flowers and some dramatic foliage to create this artful arrangement that allows you to enjoy the beauty of these exotic blooms forever.

You will need

- large rectangular container, about 15cm (6in) tall, 20cm (8in) wide and 10cm (4in) deep
- Oasis foam
- Oasis adhesive
- moss
- bent wire pins (optional)
- 6 clumps of cymbidium leaves
- 5 white moth orchids

Sylvia says ...

Although I do try to be true to nature in my arrangements, sometimes I like to mix things up a little. In this display I've combined the leaves of cymbidium orchids with the flowers of moth orchids. Although the large, fleshy leaves of the phalaenopsis are dramatic in their own right (see above), I like the way the slender, spiky cymbidium leaves break up the starkness of the moth orchid stems.

①

Fill your chosen container with Oasis foam. Secure it in place using Oasis adhesive. Then take some moss and arrange this over the top of the Oasis, so that all the foam is concealed. You can use the adhesive to secure the moss, or insert bent wire pins to hold it down.

②

Take four of the cymbidium leaf clumps and push these in to the foam at the centre of the container; place two clumps at the back, and two at the front. Position the clumps at the back slightly further apart than the two clumps at the front.

③

Take the remaining two clumps of cymbidium leaves and push one in on either side of the clumps you inserted in step 2. Position these so that they are angled slightly outwards. Take one orchid stem and insert it in roughly the centre of the display.

④

Take two more orchid stems and insert these on either side of the first orchid. Arrange each one so that the flowers flop to either side and so that the blooms face forwards. Do not position them too close to the first orchid or the arrangement will look cramped.

⑤

Take one orchid stem and push it in to the foam towards the front of the display and positioned between the centre orchid and the one on the left. Take the last orchid and insert this towards the front, and positioned between the centre orchid and the one on the right. Push the stems of these two orchids in to the foam a little deeper than you have with the other orchids – or trim the stems so that they are slightly shorter. Angle the blooms so that they fall forwards and face outwards.

Sylvia says ...

If you want to make your arrangement even more secure, dip the ends of the plant stems in to Oasis adhesive before you push them in to the foam. When the adhesive dries, the flowers will be held in place, although this means that if you want to re-use the stems you will have to cut off the glued ends.

Design ideas

For a more eye-catching display, why not use more colourful orchids? Blooms come in many shades of pink – from pale and subtle, through to bright and vivid. Or you could try one of the more multicoloured varieties (see left).

WILD AT HEART

White Queen Anne's lace, purple verbena and wispy tails of fountain grass are mixed together with the silvery foliage of sage, eucalyptus and lavender in a beautiful arrangement that combines the beauty of garden flowers with the charms of wild hedgerow plants.

You will need

- large oval tin container, about 20cm (8in) tall, 30cm (12in) wide and 15cm (6in) deep
- Oasis
- Oasis adhesive
- moss
- bent wire pins (optional)
- 1 honeysuckle stem, trimmed in to 3 or 4 sections
- 4 eucalyptus branches
- sprigs of sage
- sprigs of rosemary foliage
- 4 white cow parsley stems
- 3 cat's tail grass stems
- 4 Star of Bethlehem stems
- 10–12 long lavender stems
- 1 cow parsley stem (in bud)
- 7 purple verbena stems
- 3 Queen Anne's lace flowerheads, dyed purple (see page 123)

1

Fill your container with Oasis foam and secure it in place using Oasis adhesive. Then take some moss and arrange this over the top of the Oasis, so that all the foam is concealed. You can use adhesive to secure the moss to the Oasis, or use some bent wire pins to hold it down.

2

Insert the honeysuckle stems in the centre of the container, across the width. Push in two eucalyptus branches towards the left-hand side, and two towards the right-hand side. Fill in all around the sides of the container with sprigs of sage – push them in at an angle so they fall forwards over the edge of the container. Leave a gap at centre front. Then fill in across the centre with rosemary sprigs; make sure the sprigs at the very centre are taller and that those towards the sides fan outwards.

Sylvia says ...

This is one of my favourite arrangements – I love the combination of the purple flowers and the silvery eucalyptus, sage and rosemary foliage. It's hard to specify exactly how much greenery to use here – I just keep adding sprigs of foliage until the display is as I want it. The fuller the pot, the better!

3

Take two of the cow parsley stems and insert these near the centre of the container; make sure that one stem is the tallest point in the display. Push in one cow parsley stem at the front of the container, towards the left-hand side; push the remaining stem in at the right-hand side. Arrange the cow parsley stems so that they fan outwards. Take a few of the leaves from the cat's tail grass and insert these at the very heart of the display.

4

Insert one Star of Bethlehem stem at the centre of the arrangement; push the stem in so that the flowerhead is roughly in the middle of the display and facing forwards. Push in another Star of Bethlehem a little behind the first; angle this flower so that it faces towards the back of the display and stands a little taller than the first. Add the remaining two Star of Bethlehem stems on either side of the first pair, so that they are angled outwards and their blooms face forwards. Push in the lavender stems at the centre of the display; make the stems at the centre the tallest point in the display and angle the lower ones outwards.

5

Push the budding cow parsley stem in at the centre of the display; this is now the highest point. Add two cat's tail grasses in front of this, on either side of the central Star of Bethlehem stem, and angled so that they fall forwards. Push in the remaining cat's tail grass at the centre-back.

6

Take a piece of verbena and push it in to the gap at the centre-front of the arrangement. Take two of the purple-dyed Queen Anne's lace and add these at the centre, on either side of the verbena. Add the remaining dyed Queen Anne's lace at the centre-back. Then fill in the display with the remaining stems of purple verbena, spacing them evenly throughout the arrangement and angling the stems so that the flowers face outwards.

WHITE DELIGHT

The everlasting charm of the rose lies at the heart of this magnificent display. Old Roses and English Roses are mixed together with a mass of other white and cream flowers, and then set against an array of different shades of green – sprays of skimmia, sprigs of sage, honeysuckle and hop bines.

You will need

- large oval basket, about 25cm (10in) tall, 30cm (12in) wide and 25cm (10in) deep
- Oasis foam
- Oasis adhesive
- moss
- bent wire pins (optional)
- 8 skimmia stems
- 4 stems of camellia foliage
- 4 sprigs of sage
- 2 hop branches
- 1 stem of hollyhock buds
- 2 white hydrangea stems
- 3 pale green viburnum stems
- 3 honeysuckle stems
- 4 large white Old roses
- 3 sprays of white Floribunda roses

Sylvia says ...

When the handle broke on my old-fashioned, wicker, shopping basket, the base of the basket was still sound and I knew I would be able to transform it in to the perfect container for a wonderful display. All I had to do was trim off the broken handle and then fill the basket with Oasis foam, topped off with moss.

1

Fill the basket with Oasis foam and secure it with adhesive. Cover the foam with moss and secure it in place with adhesive or bent wire pins. Take one of the skimmia stems and insert it at the centre-back of the display. Push in two camellia stems, one on either side of the skimmia and angling them so that they fan outwards. This is the foliage background for the arrangement.

2

Push in a sprig of sage on either side of the display, angled forwards over the edge of the basket. Push the other two sage sprigs in at the back, positioned in front of the foliage background and on either side of the first skimmia stem.

3

Insert four skimmia stems along the front of the basket; push the stems in to the Oasis foam at an angle so that the skimmia falls forwards over the basket edge. Push in the remaining three skimmia stems towards the back of the display, in front of the foliage background and positioned so that one skimmia is at the centre, flanked by the remaining two stems.

4

Add the hop branches towards the back of the display. Position one branch on either side of the centre point and take care not to push the stems in too far – the hops should now add height to the display.

5

Take the stem of hollyhock buds and push it in at the centre-back. Take the two white hydrangea stems and add these at the centre-front of the display; push the stems in at a slight angle and make sure that the large, glossy leaves fall forwards over the edge of the basket.

6

Take two of the viburnum stems and push in at the right-hand side. Position one stem quite low down, so that it falls down over the edge of the basket; position the other stem slightly above, but still angled outwards. Add the remaining viburnum stem to the left-hand side, positioned so the stems are angled outwards and the flowerheads droop down.

7

Add the honeysuckle stems to the centre of the display, positioning two slightly left of centre and one slightly right of centre. Do not push the stems too far in to the Oasis; the honeysuckle stems need to add some more height at the centre of the arrangement.

8

Take one of the Old roses and add to the front of the display, slightly to the left of the centre and in front of the white hydrangeas. Push the stem well in so that the bloom is low down at the front and facing outwards. Push in another Old rose behind this and to the left, keeping the flowerhead taller than the first and angled outwards. Add another Old rose to the right of the display, in a position that mirrors the one you've just put in. Push the last Old rose in at the centre-back of the display, keeping the flowerhead tall in the display and facing forward.

9

Take one spray of Floribunda roses and add to the display just to the left of the front-facing Old rose. Take another spray and push it in to the arrangement at the right, towards the front of the basket. Angle the stems so that the roses on both of these sprays face forwards and outwards. Add the last spray of roses at the very centre, placed between the outer Old roses and angled so that the flowers face upwards.

Sylvia says ...

This display features one of my favourite filler plants – hops. I love the way the delicate, pale green hop 'flowers' add texture to the greenery in an arrangement. And the spiraling tendrils at the ends of the branches help to break up the outline of the other foliage.

MEADOW POSY

Bright yellow buttercups, frothy cow parsley and delicate meadow grasses are gathered together with pale pink and dark pink ranunculus to create a perfect posy with that just-picked-from-the-countryside look. A simple pitcher is the ideal container for such a pretty display.

You will need

- 1 large enamel jug, about 30cm (12in) tall
- 10–12 clumps of meadow grass
- 4 dark pink ranuncula stems
- 2 sprays of lady's mantle
- 6 sprays of Queen Anne's lace
- 7 buttercup stems
- 7 pale pink ranunculus stems

Design ideas

This arrangement would make a wonderful – and original – bouquet for an informal wedding. First tie the flowers used in steps 1 and 2 in to a bunch. Then gather some meadow grass and buttercups around this bunch and tie again. Take the remaining flowers – as outlined in step 5 – and tie these in place around the bouquet. Then use a decorative ribbon to conceal your ties and add the finishing touch.

Take three to four clumps of meadow grass and fan out the leaves; tease the flowering stems forwards, so that they are visible between the foliage. Arrange the grass towards the back of your jug.

Take two of the dark pink ranunculi and place these at the centre-back, in amongst the meadow grass. Arrange the lady's mantle in front of the meadow grass and ranunculi, with one stem on either side. Insert one spray of Queen Anne's lace at the centre, pushing it in amongst the lady's mantle. Then take two more sprays of Queen Anne's lace and put one on the left and one on the right.

Add another stem of Queen Anne's lace at the right-hand side. Then take four or five more clumps of meadow grass and use these to fill in, all around the display.

Sylvia says ...

The beauty of this display is that it's arranged very much as if you had gathered a bunch of flowers on a walk in the fields. Since no supporting medium is used, you can rearrange the flowers as often as you like. If you do want to create a more permanent arrangement then you could place Oasis foam (see page 48) or acrylic water (see page 49) in the bottom of the container to secure the stems; if you use the latter, make sure the container is watertight. Or you could use raffia or twine to hand tie the flowers in to a bunch before putting them in the container (see page 50).

4

Now take the buttercups and push them in all around the edges so that they flop forwards over the edge of the container. Make sure you don't push in the ones at the back too far; they need to be visible through the meadow grass foliage.

5

Add the last sprays of Queen Anne's lace at the back of the display. Take the remaining dark pink ranunculi stems and add one to the left-hand side and one to the right. Angle the flowers so that they are pointing forwards. Now take the pale pink ranunculi and push them in around the lower part of the display, including the back. Make sure that the flowers at the back of the display are still visible through the rest of the arrangement.

ROMANTIC BLUES

Blue is considered to be among the most calming and peaceful of colours, so what
could be more restful than this lovely display, featuring big, beautiful agapanthus flowerheads?
Frothy white Queen Anne's lace brings a light, romantic touch to this arrangement.

You will need

- oval basket about 10cm (4in) tall, 20cm (8in) wide and 15cm (6in) deep
- Oasis foam
- Oasis adhesive
- moss
- bent wire pins (optional)
- 2 clumps of agapanthus leaves
- 6 eucalyptus stems
- 2 Queen Anne's lace flowerheads
- 5 stems of white wild clematis
- 6 stems of blue wild clematis
- 4 agapanthus flowerheads

Sylvia says ...

I often use baskets as the containers for my silk flower displays; the woven surface adds an element of texture without being too intrusive. One thing I do consider, however, is how sturdy the basket is; if it's quite lightweight then I try to make sure it's sufficiently weighed down to prevent the display from toppling over. I find that an old tile or two, placed in the bottom of the basket, just under the Oasis foam, works really well.

1 Fill the basket with Oasis foam, leaving a slight gap between the sides of the foam and the sides of the basket. Secure it in place using Oasis adhesive. Then take some moss and push it down in to the basket between the Oasis and the sides of the basket in order to hide the foam from view. Cover the top of the Oasis with moss so that the foam is concealed. You can use the adhesive to secure the moss, or insert some bent wire pins to hold it down.

2 Take the clumps of agapanthus leaves and push them in to the foam at the centre-back of the display, placing them about 2.5cm (1in) apart. Push two eucalyptus stems in front of the agapanthus leaves and towards the front of the basket, angled so that the leaves fall forwards and outwards. Push in two more eucalyptus stems at the left-hand side, positioning one facing upwards and outwards at the back, the other facing outwards at the side. Repeat with the remaining eucalyptus stems at the right-hand side.

3 Push in one Queen Anne's lace stem at the centre of the display, in between and just in front of the agapanthus leaves. Don't push the stem in to the Oasis too far – keep the flowerhead tall in the arrangement. Add the other Queen Anne's lace in front of the first, but push the stem down quite far so that the flowerhead is low in the display, facing forwards and outwards over the edge of the basket; trim the end of the stem if it's too long to achieve this position.

Sylvia says ...

You can give your display extra security by using Oasis adhesive to hold the silk flower stems in place. Dab a bit of glue on the end of the stem before you push it in to the foam. You don't have to do this with all the plants or flowers, maybe just the heavier leaves or stems.

4

Take two of the white wild clematis stems and push these in to the foam to the left of the tall Queen Anne's lace stem, placing one slightly in front of the other. Repeat with two more of the white wild clematis to the right of the tall Queen Anne's lace. Take the last piece of white wild clematis and trim in to small sections. Push these in around the front of the display on the right and left sides, angling the stems so that they fall over the edge of the basket.

5

Push in two blue wild clematis stems at the back of the display, on either side of the centre. Add another two on the left-hand side, positioned to the left of the white wild clematis and angled outwards. Add another on the right-hand side, in a similar position. Take the remaining blue wild clematis and trim in to smaller sections. Push these in all round the front of the display so that they fall outwards over the edge of the basket.

6

Take one agapanthus flowerhead and push it in to the centre so that the flower falls between the two Queen Anne's lace flowerheads, facing outwards. Take another agapanthus and insert it at the centre-back of the display, just behind the taller of the Queen Anne's lace stems. Push in one agapanthus at the left-hand side, and one at the right. Position these flowers so that they are slightly higher than the centre-front agapanthus and so that the flowerheads point outwards.

ORIENTAL MAGIC

If you want to create a truly outstanding display, then go for the brazen beauty of red amaryllis. The fiery colour of the blooms used in this arrangement will light up any room, whatever the time of day. Choose a dramatic container for a striking result.

You will need

- tall, square-shaped container, about 30cm (12in) tall and 12.5cm (5in) wide
- Oasis foam
- Oasis adhesive
- moss
- bent wire pins (optional)
- 3 clumps of moth-orchid leaves
- 5 red amaryllis
- 3 leafless beech twigs
- 4 vine tendrils

Sylvia says ...

Because this is such a precious container, and one that I want to be able to use over and over again, I didn't want to secure the Oasis foam with glue. So I found a plastic flowerpot that was the right shape to fit tightly inside the container and stuck the Oasis in that. Once the Oasis was covered with moss, the top of the plastic pot was entirely concealed.

1

Fill your chosen container with Oasis foam. Secure it in place using Oasis adhesive. Then take some moss and arrange this over the top of the Oasis, so that all the foam is concealed. You can use the adhesive to secure the moss, or insert some bent wire pins to hold it down in position.

2

Take the clumps of moth-orchid leaves and push two in at the back of the container, one in each corner. Push the remaining clump in at the centre-front of the display. Tease out some of the aerial roots that are attached to the leaf clumps so that they hang out over the edge of the pot.

3

Take one amaryllis and push it in to the foam at the centre of the display. Push the stem down, so that the flowerhead is about 15cm (6in) above the edge of the container (trim off the end of the flower stem if necessary). Add another amaryllis to the left of the arrangement; push the stem in at an angle but twist it so that the flower faces outwards. Position the flower at about the same height as the first one.

4

Push two more amaryllis in to the centre of the Oasis, just behind the centre-front flower. Angle the stems so that they face outwards, one to the left and one to the right. These flowerheads should be positioned slightly higher than the centre-front amaryllis. Put in another amaryllis at the centre-back, positioned so that this flower is the highest of the five blooms.

5

Push one of the beech twigs in to the arrangement at the left, to one side of the central clump of flowers. Push another beech twig in at the back of the display, making sure it is visible above and between the flowers.

6

Push in the remaining beech twig at the back, to the right-hand side. Take one vine tendril and push it in to the foam just to the left of the central group of amaryllis; twist the tendril around so that it falls forwards over the edge of the pot. Push a tendril in to the foam at roughly the same position but twist this one so that it points upwards. Add the remaining two tendrils on the other side of the container, mirroring the position of the first pair.

Sylvia says ...

Silk amaryllis stems are bare of foliage and for this display I wanted something at the base of the flowers that would fan out over the edges of the container. Clumps of leaves that come with moth orchids were the ideal solution, but I could just as easily have chosen aspidistra leaves for an equally dramatic look. You can, of course, do without leaves at all, or substitute another kind of foliage.

WINTER WARMTH

The warmth of the burgundy-red hellebores and ranunculi in this display form a
perfect contrast with the cool shades of pale green lady's mantle and silvery eucalyptus foliage.
The use of such complementary colours will brighten any corner.

You will need

- shallow, round ceramic dish, about 25cm (10in) in diameter
- Oasis foam
- Oasis adhesive
- moss
- bent wire pins (optional)
- 2 eucalyptus branches
- 3 honeysuckle stems
- 1 cow parsley stem
- 3 small stems of lady's mantle
- 3 stems of deep burgundy-red hellebores
- 3 deep burgundy-red ranunculi

1 Fill your chosen dish with Oasis foam. Secure it in place using a suitable adhesive. Take some moss and arrange this over the top of the Oasis so that all the foam is concealed. You can use adhesive to secure the moss or insert some bent wire pins to hold it down.

2 Cut the eucalyptus in to eight smaller sections. Arrange in a circle in the centre, with the leaves fanning out and so the leaves at the back are higher than those at the front. Cut the flowerless stems off the honeysuckle and insert at the back, fanning out from the centre.

3 Take one of the flowering honeysuckle stems and insert this at the centre-back. Add the cow parsley stem, pushing it in just next to honeysuckle. Insert another flowering honeysuckle stem at the left-hand side of the arrangement; add the remaining one to the right. Angle both of these so that they fan very slightly outwards from the centre.

Sylvia says ...

You don't have to use silk flowers 'as they come'. I often trim stems in to smaller sections, especially those that feature many branches and that offer lots of foliage. In this display, I've snipped off the honeysuckle stems that don't bear flowers and used these separately. This is also a great way to get the most value from the silk flowers you buy.

4

Insert one stem of lady's mantle in to the centre of the display, positioning the flowerhead so that it's in the middle of the flowers. Insert another lady's mantle at the front of the container, just left of centre; insert the remaining lady's mantle just to the right of centre. Push these two stems well in to the Oasis so that the flowerheads are placed low down in the display and fall forwards over the edge of the dish.

5

Add one of the hellebore stems at the centre-back of the display – keep it in a tall position but not as high as the flowering honeysuckle stems. Snip off a bud from one of the remaining hellebore stems and push it in to the gap at the centre-front of the dish. Add one hellebore stem on the right-hand side, and the remaining hellebore on the left. Push their stems in to the foam at an angle so that the flowers fan outwards and the flowers fall slightly downwards.

Design ideas

Hellebores – also known as Lenten roses – come in unusual dusky shades, such as the deep burgundy red used in this display. But they are also sold in white, as do ranunculi. If you want to create a lighter, brighter display, try the white versions of these key silk flowers.

6

Push one of the ranunculi in to the very centre of the arrangement, just below the upper hellebore stem. Add another ranunculi just to the right of the first one, and another just to the left. The ranunculi should all be roughly on the same level.

MY HEART'S EASE

Heartsease, or wild pansies, are long-time cottage-garden favourites.
A mass of these perennially popular plants – set in a wide, shallow container –
is full of old-world charm that is guaranteed to win anyone's heart.

You will need

- 1 large oval tin, about 12.5cm (5in) tall, 30cm (12in) wide and 10cm (4in) deep
- Oasis foam
- Oasis adhesive
- moss
- bent wire pins (optional)
- 7 pansy bunches

1

Fill your chosen container with Oasis foam. Secure it in place using a suitable adhesive. Take some moss and arrange over the top of the Oasis, so that all the foam is concealed. You can use adhesive to secure the moss, or insert some bent wire pins to hold it down.

2

Take one pansy bunch and push it in at the centre-front of the container. Push another bunch in directly behind. Take a third bunch and divide it in to two smaller bunches. Push these in to the front of the display on either side of the centre-front pansies.

3

Take one pansy bunch and push it in to the container at the left-hand side. Push another bunch in at the right-hand side.

4

Use one pansy bunch to fill in the gap between the left-hand pansies and the central clump of flowers. Use the remaining bunch of pansies to fill in the last gap to the right of the centre of the arrangement.

PERFECT POMPOMS

Sometimes the simplest of designs create the greatest impact. Alliums – with
their pleasing pompom flowerheads in white or shades of purple – are perfect statement plants.
It takes just a few of these blooms – plus a handful of leaves – to make a dramatic display.

You will need

- cylindrical glass vase, about 20cm (8in) tall and 20cm (8in) in diameter
- Oasis foam
- Oasis adhesive
- moss
- bent wire pins (optional)
- 2–4 anthurium leaves
- 4 clumps of allium leaves
- 8 individual allium leaves
- 3 white allium
- 2 purple allium

Sylvia says ...

Lining a glass vase with large leaves is an ideal way to conceal the Oasis foam that you are using. You can use any leaves you like – aspidistra and hydrangea leaves are particularly good for this purpose. If you ever trim off any leaves from flowering stems, don't discard them; set them aside for this very purpose on future displays.

1

Fill the glass vase with Oasis foam, leaving a slight gap between the foam and the side of the vase. Secure in place using a suitable adhesive. Then take the anthurium leaves and slip them in to the container, between the Oasis and the side of the vase. Insert the base of the leaves first. Fold or trim off the tops of the leaves so that they are level with the top of the vase. Conceal the top of the Oasis with moss, securing it with adhesive or some wire pins.

2

Take two clumps of allium leaves and insert at the centre of the Oasis. Dab the ends of the leaves with a little Oasis adhesive before pushing them in to the foam to help secure them more effectively in position.

3

Insert the remaining two clumps of allium leaves. Position them close to – and just in front of – the ones you have just used. As in step 2, secure the ends of these with a dab of Oasis glue.

4

Take one of the white alliums and push it in to the Oasis at the centre, just in front of the leaves. Twist the stem so that the flower bends slightly forwards and outwards. Push another white allium in at the centre-back, behind the leaves. Twist the stem of this flower so that it bends slightly backwards and outwards. Make sure this flower is higher than the first. Push in the remaining white allium to the right of the centre. Twist the stem so that the flower bends slightly out and to the left. Push the stem in to the Oasis so that the flower is the lower of the three.

5

Take one of the purple alliums and push it in at the centre, just to the left of the central clump of leaves. Angle it slightly to the left. Push in the remaining purple allium to the right of centre. Angle this one so that it bends outwards, towards the right of the display.

CHRISTMAS WREATH

In the darkest days of winter, it's traditional to bring light in to the home to celebrate
the turning of the season and bring hope of longer days to come. Bring this glowing wreath
to your Christmas table, set a candle at its centre, and illuminate your festivities.

You will need

- Oasis ring, about 30cm (12in) across
- 1 stem of variegated ivy leaves
- 6 ivy flowers
- 10 rose-hip sprigs
- 8–9 dark red roses
- storm lantern
- white candle

Design ideas

A silk flower wreath makes an ideal centrepiece for any celebratory table throughout the year. Use small dahlia flowers in shades of red and orange, teamed with artichoke buds for an autumnal table display. Combine sweet peas with verbena and anemones for a colourful summer wreath. And mix hyacinths with narcissi for a spring celebration.

1 This display is created directly in to an Oasis foam ring rather than in a container. The stems of the silk flowers are pushed in to the foam ring and then the ring can be placed on a plate or tray to display. If using this kind of ring, make sure you cover the foam completely with flowers and foliage.

2 Cut the ivy stem in to seven or eight shorter lengths and push these in to the Oasis ring, spacing them evenly around the ring. Trim off about eight foliage sprigs from the roses and push these in to the ring too, spacing them evenly.

3 Push the ivy flowers in to the ring, spacing them evenly all round. Push some in to the outside edge of the ring, so that they face outwards; push some in to the top side of the ring, facing upwards; push some in to the inside of the ring, facing inwards.

4

Push the rose hips in to the Oasis ring. Insert some in to the outside edge of the ring so that they face outwards and turn slightly downwards. Push some in to the top edge of the ring, facing upwards and slightly in towards the centre.

5

Trim the dark red rose stems to about 7.5cm (3in) long and remove any leaves. Push the flowers in around the Oasis, filling in the gaps on the sides and on the top of the foam ring.

6

This display looks wonderful with a candle at the centre. But for safety's sake, it is vital that an unprotected candle and naked flame are not placed inside the wreath. Place the candle in a storm lantern or tall, heatproof glass container to avoid the risk of fire.

CHAPTER 4

Silk flowers for special occasions

To celebrate a grand wedding, a baby shower or just a truly special day, mark the occasion with an everlasting silk flower display that ensures the occasion is remembered for many years to come.

VALENTINE'S DAY BOUQUET

Stunning roses with tightly packed, soft, curling petals in the palest shades of peach
and lilac are the feature of this gorgeous romantic arrangement. The refined colours of
the roses are set against the dark green leaves and combined with delicate, twiggy birch
stems to create a love-enhancing bouquet.

You will need

- 9 pale pink roses
- 3 pale lilac roses
- 6 birch twigs (with budding leaves)
- florists' tape or raffia
- wide, burgundy-coloured, wired ribbon

Sylvia says ...

I've used wired ribbon to bind around the finished bunch of roses and hide the florists' tape that holds the whole arrangement together. A fine length of wire runs along the edges of the ribbon, concealed within a narrow hem. The wire can be bent in to shape, making it possible to create bows that remain stiff and upright.

1 Take three of the pale pink roses and one of the pale lilac roses. Carefully group the stems together so that the pale lilac rose is at the centre. Add three of the birch twigs to one side of the bunch. Use florists' tape or raffia to bind the bunch together.

2 Use three more of the pale pink roses, one of the pale lilac roses and three more of the birch twigs to create another tied bunch, as in step 1. Repeat once more with the remaining flowers and twigs to make a third tied bunch.

3 Group the three bunches together, arranging them so that the birch twigs are on the outside of the bunch. Use florists' tape or raffia to bind all three bunches together. Take a length of wired ribbon and wrap around the bunch. Tie in a bow and bend the wired edges of the ribbon so that the bow stands proud of the flowers.

HEN PARTY BAGS

When you're celebrating forthcoming nuptials, what could
be a more delightful way to remember the occasion than with these
charming party gifts? Bold and beautiful pink and white peonies are tied
in to bunches and then presented in contrasting paper gift bags.

You will need

To make one party bag:

- 2 white peonies, including buds
- 6 pale magenta peonies, including buds
- raffia
- pink tissue paper
- square, green bag made from stiff paper

Sylvia says ...

Because you don't have to worry about keeping these gorgeous silk peonies in water, you can use simple paper bags to present your gifts. And when your girlfriends get home, the bags are still stylish enough to display as pretty containers for their bachelorette bouquets.

1 Take one white and three pale magenta peonies and group in to a loose bunch. Make sure you include peony buds in the bunch. Use raffia to tie the stems together; position the raffia low down and tie it tightly – this will cause the flowerheads to spread out slightly.

2 Take the remaining peonies and tie in to another bunch, as in step 1. Cut a piece of pink tissue paper big enough to line the bag that you are using. Slip it in to the bag so that it lines the sides.

3 Take the two tied bunches and lower them in to the bag, with their stems inside the tissue-paper lining. Arrange the flowers so that they sit proud of the top edge of the bag. Knot the rope handle of the bag for an additional decorative touch if wished.

THE ANNIVERSARY DINNER

When you are creating silk flower displays for a celebration meal, you want something that issimple, yet striking. These elegant arrangements look stylish set along the length of a rectangular table, or grouped together at the centre of a circular one.

You will need

- 3 white viburnum stems
- 3 matching bud vases, each about 30cm (12in) tall
- 3 Queen Anne's lace stems
- 12 cat's tail grass leaves
- 6 white hellebores
- 9 cream freesias
- 9 white roses

Sylvia says ...

I chose bud vases for these displays, since their slender shape was particularly elegant. However, bud vases have rather narrow necks at the top, so if you find it a struggle to insert the flowers in to your chosen vases, try binding the stems together tightly before putting them in.

1 Put one viburnum stem in to each vase. If you want to secure the stems in the vases you could use some acrylic water (see page 49). Oasis will not work so well in such narrow vases – if you try to cut the foam to fit such in to a small space, it will crumble.

2 Put one stem of Queen Anne's lace in to each vase. Push the stem well down in to the vase so that the flowerhead is just above the top of the vase. Add four grass leaves to each vase; arrange them so that they droop outwards, two on either side of the display.

3 Add two hellebores to each vase; keep one facing upwards and angle the other so that the flower faces outwards and downwards. Add two freesias to each vase; bend or twist the stems so that the flowers fan outwards at the bottom of the display. Add another freesia to the centre of each arrangement.

4 Add one white rose to each vase, positioning each flower so that it sits just above the Queen Anne's lace. Add the final two roses to each arrangement, positioning these on either side of the first rose and so that all three rose flowers are roughly the same height.

WEDDING TOP TABLE

A wedding is one of life's happiest occasions and should be celebrated in style. This spectacular display makes the ideal centrepiece. Combined with smaller arrangements and a hand-tied bouquet, it's the crowning glory of that most special of days.

You will need

- 1 lattice of budding twigs
- heavy glass vase, about 1m (1yd) tall and 25cm (10in) in diameter at top
- flat plastic plate or dish that rests comfortably on the top of the tall vase
- Oasis foam
- Oasis adhesive
- 8 honeysuckle stems, without flowers
- 2 stems of camellia foliage, cut in to smaller sections
- 6 large white peonies, with foliage
- 3 cow parsley stems
- 2 cherry blossom stems
- 3 stems of white wild clematis
- 2 white viburnum stems

Sylvia says ...

When I first made this display – for my son's wedding – I wanted to set it on top of a tall, glass vase so that the whole arrangement had height and impact. But on its own, the vase seemed rather dull. I then hit upon the idea of filling it with a lattice of simple artificial twigs. Instantly, the twigs added a delicate criss-cross pattern to the glass vase that seemed the perfect foil for the main display.

1

Form the lattice of budding twigs in to a cylindrical shape. Slip this in to the vase. Place the second container on top of the vase; it should cover the opening of the vase without protruding too much on either side. Place Oasis foam on top of the plate and glue in place; trim off any foam that sticks out over the edge of the plate. You will be inserting flowers in to the side and top of the Oasis.

2

Insert four honeysuckle stems in to the Oasis: place two left of centre and two right of centre, fanning out slightly. Push in another honeysuckle stem at the bottom-left so that it trails down; repeat at the bottom-right. Push a honeysuckle stem in to the left side so that it sticks out at a right angle; repeat on the right side. Insert pieces of camellia foliage around the bottom front edge. Trim six leafed stems from the peonies and insert at the back, fanning up and out.

3

Take one cow parsley stem and push it in to the centre-front: push well in so that it the flowers are 10–15cm (4–6in) above the top of the foam. Push another cow parsley stem in to the centre of the left-hand side of the block, positioned so that it falls downwards and outwards. Repeat with the remaining cow parsley stem on the right side of the block.

4

Push one of the cherry blossom stems in to the top of the Oasis, about 2.5cm (1in) in from the left-hand edge. Angle the stem so that it tilts very slightly outwards. Keep the stem tall in the display, but not as tall as the honeysuckle. Repeat with the remaining cherry blossom stem on the right-hand side of the Oasis.

5

Push one wild clematis stem in to the top of the Oasis, about 2.5cm (1in) from the centre-back. Keep the stem upright and roughly as tall as the honeysuckle stems. Add another wild clematis stem to the left-hand side; push it down and angle the stem at 45 degrees so that the flowers fan outwards. Push another wild clematis stem in to the right-hand side; push this one upwards in to the foam so that the flowers are angled downwards.

6

Push one white viburnum stem in to the right-hand side, at right angles and just above the last piece of wild clematis you put in. Cut the remaining viburnum in to individual flowerheads: push two in to the top, one on the right and one on the left. Push them in well so the flowers are 5cm (2in) above the foam, and angled to face outwards. Push the remaining viburnum flowers in to the front, angled upwards so the flowers face down.

Sylvia says …

To create an even more impressive display, set this centrepiece on a mirror. This serves to double the beauty of the flowers and to reflect light up under the arrangement. You can use any mirror that you like, although I find an unframed mirror works best. Just make sure that it's spotlessly clean and completely stable before you place your display on top.

7

Push one white peony in to the front of the Oasis, just left of centre and above the viburnum flowers added at the end of step 6. Angle the stem so the flower faces upwards: don't push it in too far – the flower has to stand out further than the viburnums. Take another peony and push it in to the front about 2.5cm (1in) from the right-hand edge, positioned at the same height as the first.

8

Push in another peony at the front, between the peonies added in step 7, and at the same height. Push another peony in to the top-centre, 7.5cm (3in) above the last one added. Add another two peonies on either side, at the same height and angled outwards. Push these last peonies in to the left and right sides, level with the lower peonies and facing out. Fill any gaps with peony foliage.

INDIVIDUAL TABLE TOPPERS

You will need

- 9 small, white Tea roses, with foliage
- 9 small, cream Tea roses, with foliage
- raffia
- 3 round glass vases, each about 7.3cm (3in) in diameter at the opening
- acrylic water
- florists' tape

1

Gather together three white roses and three cream roses. Arrange them in to a pleasing bunch, with most of the foliage on the outside. Bind the stems together with raffia. Repeat with the remaining roses to make two more bunches.

2

The bunches of roses need to sit in your chosen vases with the leaves and flowers just falling over the edge. Trim off the ends of the bunched stems so that each bunch fits neatly in its vase. Mix up some acrylic water (see page 49) according to the manufacturer's instructions and pour in to the vases until they are about one-third full.

3 ————————————

Stretch two lengths of florists' tape across the top of one vase, leaving a gap between the two pieces. Stretch another two lengths across the vase in the opposite direction, so that the tapes are at right angles to the first two lengths. Again, leave a gap between the two pieces. You should have a small, square gap at the centre of the vase opening, framed by the four pieces of florists' tape. Repeat with the other two vases.

4 ————————————

Insert the stems of the roses through the central gap in the florists' tape and push down so that the base of the stems are submerged in the acrylic water. The florists' tape will support the flowers while the acrylic water sets. Put the other two bunches in to their vases in the same way. Following the manufacturer's instructions, put aside to let the acrylic water set – usually 48 hours. When the acrylic water has set, peel off the tape.

BRIDAL BOUQUET

You will need

- 12 white Tea roses
- 12 cream Tea roses
- 3 short stems of skimmia
- raffia or florists' wire
- elastic band
- white ribbon

Sylvia says ...

I've chosen white and cream flowers for these arrangements since these are so often the colours of choice at a wedding. However, if you're creating displays for a wedding with a different colour scheme it's a simple matter to adapt these table decorations. Peonies and roses – the key flowers here – come in a range of colours, or you could substitute completely different flowers. If in doubt, look at the Silk Flower Directory at the beginning of this book for ideas.

1

Take three white roses and three cream roses and gather them together in a bunch with one of the skimmia stems. Arrange the stems so that the skimmia and most of the rose leaves are to one side of the bunch. Tie the bunch together securely with a length of raffia or florists' wire.

2

Repeat step 1 with the remaining flowers to make two more similar-looking bunches. Trim off the stems so that they are even at the end. Gather the three bunches together to make one bigger bunch; secure them together temporarily with an elastic band.

3

Turn the bouquet over so you can see the right side – the side that will be facing outwards when carried by the bride. Check that you are happy with the way the bunches are grouped; holding the bouquet in front of you and looking in a mirror is an ideal way to do this. Then bind the three bunches together with raffia or florists' wire; remove the elastic band. Wind the white ribbon round and round the stems so that they are completely concealed. Tie the ribbon to secure and either cut off the loose ends or finish with a decorative bow.

BABY SHOWER ROSES

Miniature cream roses, set in a pretty pink or blue gingham container, make a charming gift for any mother-to-be. Each spray of roses is smothered in tiny blooms and set off by a mass of dark green foliage, making this arrangement easy to create, yet oh-so effective.

You will need

- square-shaped tin container, about 15cm (10in) tall and 10cm (8in) wide
- Oasis foam
- Oasis adhesive
- 3 sprays of miniature cream roses

Sylvia says ...

Silk flowers make the perfect floral gift since they last forever. Create this pretty arrangement for any baby shower and it is guaranteed to be enjoyed for many years. Pick a container in pastel colours and the flowers could be the ideal decoration for a nursery!

1

Place a block of Oasis foam inside the container. The foam need only fit the container roughly; it doesn't need to be too snug a fit. The top of the foam should be about 5cm (2in) below the top edge of the container. Secure the bottom of the foam to the container with the adhesive.

2

Before you begin, it is a good idea to lightly steam the flowers. Holding at the end of the stem, place the flower over a steaming kettle for a few seconds, then remove from the heat. Gently tease open the flowers and tweak the leaves in to shape with your fingertips. Pull the branches of each spray so that each one has a more open appearance. Push one spray in to the top of the Oasis towards the centre-front. Angle the stem so that the flowers face forward and some of the foliage falls over the front.

3

Take one of the other rose sprays and push it in to the Oasis foam towards the back and left of the container. Angle the stem so that spray faces slightly outwards towards the left. Repeat with the remaining rose spray, angling this stem outwards and towards the right. Make sure all three rose sprays are placed at roughly the same height.

MOTHER'S DAY TREAT

Three single hydrangea sprigs, in soft shades, look a treat arranged in small glass vases;
the ideal decorative finish to a tea tray. So go ahead and spoil your mum on Mother's Day – make
her these simple arrangements that she'll be able to cherish for many a year.

You will need

- 3 round glass vases, each about 7.3cm (3in) in diameter at the opening
- 9 meadow grass leaves
- acrylic water
- 3 small hydrangeas, with foliage attached

Sylvia says ...

Although these round glass vases are the ideal setting for such a simple display, I thought that they needed something extra. Filling them with a few leaves taken from artificial meadow grass clumps was the ideal solution. The grasses form a random spiral pattern on the inside of the vase.

1 Take one meadow grass leaf and wrap it loosely round two or three of your fingers, hold the ends down with your thumb. Put your fingers and thumb in to one of the vases and let go of the grass; it should spring outwards, up against the edge of the vase. Repeat with two more meadow grass leaves.

2 Prepare acrylic water (see page 49), following the manufacturer's instructions, and pour it in to the vase until one-third full. Put one hydrangea in to the vase and set aside for the recommended period until the acrylic water is set. Use florists' tape stretched across the top of the vase to hold the hydrangea in place (see page 110).

3 Repeat step 1 to insert three more meadow grass leaves in the remaining two vases. Fill these with acrylic water as in step 2 and add the remaining hydrangeas. Make sure the leaves point outwards, over the rims of the vases.

ANNIVERSARY AMARYLLIS

Amaryllis, with their wide, open, trumpet-shaped flowers, are both elegant and exotic.
Each stem bears several flowers, so using only a few amaryllis can create a dramatic
and impressive display. A gift of these memorable flowers is the ideal way to
mark any significant occasion.

You will need

- large, glass, goblet-shaped vase, about 30cm (12in) tall and 20cm (8in) in diameter at the rim
- acrylic water
- florists' tape
- 5 white amaryllis

Sylvia says ...

Amaryllis look magnificent on their own, but they can still look just as good in a mixed arrangement. And since the stems of silk amaryllis are waterproof, you can combine them with fresh flowers and foliage in a vase filled with water.

① Following the manufacturer's instructions, mix up some acrylic water (see page 49) and fill the vase to nearly half way. Check the sides of the vase above the water-line for splashes or drops of the acrylic water. Wipe these off with clean cloth – once the acrylic water sets it will be impossible to remove such imperfections.

② Stretch two strips of florists' tape across the top of the vase, from front to back, spaced 5cm (2in) apart. Trim the amaryllis stems to 30–35cm (12–14in) long so that the flowerheads are clustered just above the top of the vase. Put two amaryllis in to the vase between the two strips of tape. Let one stem fall to the left and one to the right. Stretch two more strips of tape across the vase in the opposite direction, one on either side of the amaryllis.

③ Add the remaining amaryllis stems, with two in the front and one at the back. Let the stems lean sideways and use the florists' tape as support. Set the display aside somewhere that it won't be disturbed and leave to set according to the manufacturer's instructions. Carefully peel off the tape from the vase.

CHAPTER 5

Cleaning and storing silk flowers

Silk flowers need little attention once you have created your display, but in this chapter you'll find all the know-how you need to keep them in tip-top condition. You'll also find advice on how to adapt arrangements and extend the use and interest of your flowers for future display.

ADAPTING ARRANGEMENTS

The beauty of silk flowers is that you can use them over and over again. They are easy to adapt and refashion for new displays.

When you are putting together an arrangement, the silk flowers that form the focal point are often the last ones that you add after the background of foliage and filler plants. An easy way to give new life to an existing arrangement is to take out the key flowers and replace them – the background 'ingredients' can remain the same. The flowers that you substitute do not have to be the same colour but they should be a similar size if they are to fill the same space. For maximum flexibility, don't use adhesive on the stems of the key flowers so that you can easily remove them from the Oasis foam.

An interesting way to adapt an arrangement is to use a seasonal theme. In spring, for example, you can combine alliums, hyacinths or tulips as your key plants; in summer it could be roses, agapanthus or poppies with the same background plants; in autumn it might be hydrangeas or dahlias; and in winter you could use artichokes and a selection of seasonal berries and seedheads.

You can also augment your display with real, fresh flowers and foliage. The stems of silk flowers are waterproof and so you can moisten the Oasis foam with water and insert living blooms – just make sure that the container you are using is watertight.

You may, of course, want to completely change a display, removing all the flowers and starting afresh with the same container. With a little care, you should be able to take all the plants out and either store them for another arrangement, or use them straight away to create new displays.

If you want to re-use a container to create a new display, you don't have to discard the silk flowers used in that arrangement. You can always set them aside for use in other mixed displays, or you can re-use them straight away in a different container. To create this small, but charming, arrangement, one of the bunches of pansies from My Heart's Ease (see page 90) has been cut into smaller sprays and then placed with foliage in a terracotta flower pot.

The key silk flowers in this display are pink peonies and burgundy hydrangeas. If you remove these, you can create a new display by using different flowers in their place. The new blooms need to be roughly the same size as the peonies and hydrangeas; Old roses and viburnum might be a good combination, as would poppies and Queen Anne's lace. The colour of these new flowers shouldn't clash with the pale pinks and mauves of the background flowers and the silvery foliage, so stick with light shades of purple, pink and blue. Or for greater variety, choose white or cream blooms.

CLEANING AND STORING

If you do dismantle a silk flower display, you may well want to store the
silk flowers for use in a future project. And over time, you will probably need to
clean the individual flowers or the displays themselves.

Since silk flowers can be used over and over again, the chances are that you will need to keep them in storage at some point. Newly bought flowers will probably be packaged in plastic bags and so you can leave them where they are. Older flowers, that you are putting into storage, should be put in plastic bags. Clean the flowers before putting them away (see top right).

Ideally, you should hang the flowers, head down, in a dry and dark cupboard. If you have to store silk flowers flat in a box, refresh them with steam (see page 53) before use.

After a while, a silk flower display may gather dust and so it will be necessary to clean it. For regular cleaning, you can simply blow the dust away with a hairdryer, set on cool, or a can of compressed air. You can also use the vacuum cleaner, covered with a pair of tights to prevent the flowers being sucked into the machine.

If your silk flowers need more thorough cleaning you can use some water. Hold the flowers over the sink or lay them on the draining board. Fill a spray bottle with water and then spritz the individual flowers with water until water drops run off the flowers, carrying the dirt with them. Leave to dry on a clean white towel. Check that the flower is colour-fast by applying a drop of water to a small part first.

If the dust is a little more stubborn, you can wash the flowers in soapy water. Use a small drop of a liquid detergent designed for hand washing and mix it into a bowl of lukewarm water. Fill another bowl with clean water. Dip your flowers in the soapy water and agitate them slightly with your fingers to remove the dirt. Then shake off the dirty water and rinse in the clean water. Shake the flower and then leave to dry on a clean white towel.

This cleaning method should be suitable for most silk flowers, but you have any doubts test a small area of the flower first by dampening a petal and then blotting it dry with a clean cloth. If any colour leeches out of the silk, or if the silk wrinkles when dry, avoid washing the flowers.

It's a good idea to store silk flowers in plastic bags. Large flowers will probably need a bag each, but smaller blooms can be kept in groups. Put the flowers into the bag head first and then either tie the bag closed, around the whole flower, or tie it shut with the stem protruding. Just make sure that the flowerhead and foliage is inside the bag.

You can use the vacuum cleaner to remove dust from silk flowers. If you have a choice of power settings, select the lowest. Stretch a stocking or pair of tights over the end of the vacuum's nozzle and secure in place with string or an elastic band; this will prevent you accidentally sucking up your silk flowers and will also help to diffuse the power of the vacuum. Then vacuum the flower, holding the nozzle a short distance away from the section you are cleaning.

RENOVATION AND REPAIR

When you've had your silk flowers for a while – and especially if you've re-used them more than once – you may find that they start to show a little wear and tear. But since faux flowers are made of silk there are a few things that you can to do to give them a new lease of life.

Because faux flowers are made of a natural fabric – silk – it is easy to change their colour by dyeing them. White, cream and pale coloured blooms are best for dyeing; the darker the original flower, the harder it will be to add another hue. Use a fabric dye that is mixed with cold water and which is suitable for silk. Mix it up according to the manufacturer's instructions and pour into a non-reactive container – an old plastic pot will be ideal. Submerge the flower in the dye and set aside – the longer it's left, the stronger the colour will be. Don't forget, the dye will also affect the colour of the stem and any attached foliage, so if you want to avoid dyeing the leaves, make sure these do not go into the dye.

The easiest flowers to dye are white and cream ones. Because you are not over-dyeing one colour with another, the finished result is more likely to be true to the colour you want to achieve. Leave white cow parsley in a deep purple dye and you'll get an intense purple result.

You can use more than one dye to create some interesting effects. If you dye a white rose yellow, leave it to dry, and then dip it in a red dye for a short while, you will get a mottled orange result. If you dip it in the red dye a second time, you will increase the effect.

You can also hand paint your silk flowers. Use a suitable fabric paint – there are many available purely for painting on silk – and a fine paint brush. Be sure to apply the paint in delicate stripes or small dots. Try to keep any additional colour natural looking – follow the lines and shape of the petals – and don't make the colour too strong or too bold. Look at real plants and flowers as a reference, or check in gardening books.

Faux flowers can break sometimes; the flowers come away from the stems, the leaves fall off, petals droop and edges fray. If stems break then it is usually an easy thing to mend; you can use florists' tape to bind the two sections back together. Similarly, if branching stems or foliage fall off, you can re-attach them to the main stem with a binding of florists' tape. You can also use a drop of glue, applied with a hot-glue gun (see page 53).

Hot glue is also useful to glue flowers back in place, if they've fallen off. You can also use the glue to stick on individual petals, or any other elements, that have come off a faux flower stem.

As well as falling off, petals and leaves do sometimes fray slightly at the edges. Usually, this isn't particularly noticeable, but if the fraying becomes pronounced, you can remedy this by simply trimming off the loose threads. Use a pair of small sharp scissors – embroidery scissors are ideal for this – and carefully go around the edge of the frayed petals. Make sure you don't cut off too much or you'll ruin the look of the whole flower.

You can also use some of these repair techniques to extend and adapt your silk flowers. If you want to add some extra

The flowerhead of this silk freesia has come away from the stem, although the wire from inside the stem is still attached to the flower. To mend this, you simply slip the wire back inside the stem and then bind the two sections of stem together tightly with florists' tape.

Sylvia says...

I trimmed the stem of this pink rose for a display that I then later dismantled. Soon afterwards, I found I needed a long-stemmed pink rose for a different arrangement. So what I did was take a spare stem that I'd trimmed off another flower and bound it to the trimmed rose with florists' tape. The join was concealed within the finished flower display.

petals to a flower, or leaves to a branch of foliage, you can use the hot glue gun to stick them in place. And if you want to turn a short-stemmed bloom into a longer-stemmed flower, you can bind a length of spare flower stem to the short one.

STOCKISTS

This is a selection of the specialist stockists, garden centres and department stores
which sell silk flowers and the equipment required to arrange them.

Specialist suppliers

Easy Florist Supplies
www.easyfloristsupplies.co.uk

The Essentials Company
www.essentialscompany.co.uk

Floral Essential
www.floralessential.co.uk

GT Decorations
www.gtdecorations.com

Longacres Nursery
www.longacres.co.uk

Michael Dark Ltd
www.michaeldark.co.uk

Rays Florist
www.raysflorist.co.uk

Sylvia Hague
www.silkflowersbysylvia.com

Something Special
www.somethingspecialwholesale.co.uk

Department stores and garden centres

Hobbycraft
www.hobbycraft.co.uk

John Lewis
www.johnlewis.com

Wyevale Garden Centres
www.thegardencentregroup.co.uk

INDEX

ACKNOWLEDGEMENTS

This book would not have been possible without the wonderful Caroline Smith, who helped me to write it and style the photography. The photographs for Silk Flowers for the Home and Silk Flowers for Special Occasions were taken by the talented Elizabeth Zeschin, while the remainder are by the equally capable Simon Pask.

Seeing Dave Jones' initial designs for the book was an exciting experience, and it was a pleasure to see Louise Turpin create the finished pages with such elegance.

Thanks also go to the team at Quantum: Publisher Sarah Bloxham for her drive and vision, Managing Editor Julie Brooke for ensuring everything happened as it should, and Assistant Editor Jo Morley for supporting every stage of the process. Finally, Zarni Win and Rohana Yosuf for ensuring the book you hold in your hands was printed to the highest possible standard.

Closer to home, Jenny Freeman has always been ready to help out, and Mel Crossman for many years has given me her cheerful, practical assistance. Particular thanks go to my son, Jonathan, who sourced many of my flowers throughout Asia and Europe. Lastly but by no means least, I thank my husband, Michael, who enthusiastically backed my publishing this book and has been my mainstay throughout my career in floral design.